OF SAGEBRUSH
&
SLOT MACHINES

THIS
CURIOUS PLACE CALLED
NEVADA

Edited by: **Scott E. Casper**
Richard O. Davies

SIMON & SCHUSTER CUSTOM PUBLISHING

Cover photographs by Kenneth J. Evans, courtesy of the
Nevada Commission on Tourism.

Printed in the United States of America

10 9 8 7 6 5 4 3 2 1

ISBN 0–536–00089–1
BA 97043

 SIMON & SCHUSTER CUSTOM PUBLISHING
160 Gould Street/Needham Heights, MA 02194
Simon & Schuster Education Group

Copyright Acknowledgments

Table of Contents

Introduction

This Curious Place Called Nevada

There has been nothing ordinary about the history of the State of Nevada. Ever since it entered the Union on October 31, 1864, Nevada has meant different things to different people. It has been a place of mystery and myth, where vivid contrasts between city and wilderness assault the consciousness. Nevada came into the Union amidst a flurry of controversy, and during its subsequent history its acceptance of prostitution, easy divorce, and gambling—all recognized by state statute—produced widespread moral condemnation.

For much of its history, Nevada has been roundly criticized for its lax moral outlook. Others have commented critically upon Nevada's harsh natural environment and bleak landscape, often dismissing the State as a "vast wasteland." Mark Twain's reaction to Nevada's landscape in 1861, when he traveled west from St. Joseph, Missouri, by horse-drawn coach to take up residence in Carson City, helped establish an image that subsequent visitors would echo: "On the nineteenth day we crossed the Great American Desert—forty memorable miles of bottomless sand, into which the coach wheels sunk from six inches to a foot. . . . The road was white with the bones of oxen and horses . . . [and] the log-chains, wagon tires, and rotting wrecks of vehicles. . . . The desert was a prodigious graveyard," he said, concluding somberly, "Do not these relics suggest something of the idea of the fearful suffering and privation the early emigrants to California suffered?" Nevada, he implied, was a place to get through as fast as possible, not a place where rational persons would want to establish permanent residency. From the earliest days of settlement, residents and visitors alike have also objected to the searing heat of the summer months and the sharp winds and sub zero temperatures that visit upon much of the state in winter. Twain was especially impressed by a phenomenon locals referred to as the "Washoe Zephyr," which he identified as "a peculiarly Scriptural wind," observing that "it blows over flimsy houses, lifts single roofs occasionally, rolls up tin ones like sheet music, and now and then blows a stagecoach over and spills the passengers."

It has been, however, modern-day Nevada's willingness to embrace unsavory social customs, legacies of the "sin and vice" of the days of the mining frontier, that has produced the preponderance of the external criticism. Typical of such a viewpoint came even from one of the twentieth century's better presidents. In June of 1955, as he flew westward across Nevada heading for San Francisco, Harry S. Truman looked down upon a vast panorama of dark sagebrush and bare mountains, but what he saw was much more than a bleak landscape, as reflected in that evening's entry into his personal diary:

> Then we came to the great gambling and marriage destruction hell, known as Nevada. To look at it from the air it is just that—hell on earth. There are tiny green specks on the landscape where dice, roulette, light-of-loves, crooked poker and gambling thugs thrive. Such places should be abolished and so should Nevada. It never should have been made a State. A county in the great State of California would be too much of a civil existence for that dead and sinful territory. Think of that awful, sinful place having two Senators and a Congressman in Washington, and Alaska and Hawaii not represented. It is a travesty on our system and a disgrace to free government.

Truman softened his tone as California moved into view, noting that as his aircraft left "the hell hole of iniquity" it did so by passing over Lake Tahoe, "one of the most beautiful spots in the whole world." Apparently he did not know that nearly half of that crystal blue mountain lake lay within "that awful, sinful place." Truman was merely repeating an old refrain that began when Nevada was granted statehood in 1864 by the Lincoln administration because it might need Nevada's electoral votes in an anticipated close fall presidential election. Subsequent Nevada myth-makers sought to put a better spin on things by arguing that the Union needed the rich silver treasury of the Comstock to finance the war, but the federal government already had such access because of Nevada's territorial status. It was simply crass political expediency that precipitated Nevada's premature admission to the Union during the Civil War; the thirty-first state was, as the popular slogan portrayed on the state flag defiantly proclaims, "Battle Born." But the battle was a political one, and had it not been for the extraordinary political conditions of the Civil War, Nevada would not have gained statehood until well into the 20th century.

Nevada became a state in 1864 with fewer than 40,000 white residents. Despite the economic boom on the Comstock, Nevada lacked an adequately diversified economic base. Once the Comstock boom faded during the 1870s, the state fell into a deep and extended period of economic stagnation. After approaching 50,000 residents in 1880, the population declined with the economy, bottoming out in 1900 at just 42,335 hardy souls. Critics had taken to referring to Nevada as a "rotten borough," some even pointedly suggesting that it should have its statehood revoked and be returned ignominiously to the status of a territory.

That drastic fate did not happen, but conditions did not improve all that much until the Second World War. Not that enterprising Nevadans did not try. The economic bonanza expected from the nation's first federal reclamation project, which created the Truckee-Carson Irrigation District under legislation sponsored by Reno-based congressman Francis G. Newlands in 1902, failed to materialize. Its ardent enthusiasts, such as the influential journalist-promoter William E. Smythe, had raised expectations that hundreds of thousands of acres of western Nevada desert would be transformed into a bountiful agricultural oasis, whose crops would feed millions of Americans and give Nevada its long-desired economic base. With mineral prices depressed and reclamation failing to accomplish what its supporters promised, Nevadans seized upon what few options presented themselves. Although cattle ranching expanded significantly, it could not sustain a statewide economic renaissance. Neither could tourism, despite its steady expansion as a result of the introduction of the automobile and promotions conducted by railroads. Nevadans were often reduced to grasping at straws. From the late 1890s until World War I, the state hosted a steady procession of highly publicized prizefights, but at a high cost. Major bouts were staged in Reno, Goldfield, and Tonopah and attracted many out-of-state sports fans who spent money liberally, but this was a time when public moralists almost universally condemned the blood sport, which was banned in most states. Nevada thus captured national attention by endorsing a sport of most dubious reputation—the first of several times when it would defy conventional morality.

When several states legalized boxing during the 1920s in response to changing national attitudes resulting from the advent of mass spectator sports, Nevada had to seek another small niche. It did so by rewriting its divorce laws, lowering the residency requirement to three months in 1927 and to just six weeks in 1931. An economic boomlet ensued after several movie stars and other prominent individuals obtained speedy divorces in Reno. While critics interpreted the state's action as an assault upon the institution of marriage, several lawyers developed thriving practices by devoting themselves almost exclusively to providing legal services for thousands of women (and a much smaller number of men) who each year spent several weeks living in local hotels, or if they had the financial wherewithal, at plush dude ranches located on the edge of town. In 1931 4,745 divorces were granted in Reno, a number that reached 5,884 in 1945. A flurry of newspaper and magazine articles appeared each year that linked Reno's emergence as "The Divorce Capital of the Nation" with the town's unwillingness to shut down the notorious "Stockade"—a thriving prostitution district—located near the railroad tracks just north of the small central business district. Many of these sensational articles also featured the comment of flamboyant mayor E. E. Roberts, who once quipped to a reporter that he saw nothing wrong with Reno's moral outlook, suggesting that further improvements could be made: "I should like to see Reno with a whiskey barrel and a tin cup on every street corner."

It was within the historical context of such liberal attitudes, deeply rooted in the not-so-distant frontier era, that Nevada legalized gambling in 1931. The State Legislature did so to raise desperately needed tax revenues during the Great Depression. The Legislature passed the most important law in the state's history without much of a fuss, because the majority of Nevadans interpreted the law as merely recognizing the reality that gambling—a cultural legacy of the state's early mining days—was commonly practiced throughout the state. Cynics commented that the legislature's action would merely make it possible for locals to enjoy their card and dice games without having to pay off local politicians and law enforcement officers; if the state could pick up a few thousand dollars in license fees, so much the better. Opposition did emerge, primarily from the Women's Christian Temperance Union, the Nevada Federation of Women's Clubs, and the Mormon and Methodist churches. Their claims that legalized gambling would put the government in the position of undercutting community morality proved inadequate. After Republican Governor Fred Balzor signed the bill into law, the only immediate consequence was that the gaming tables and slot machines were moved from the basements and back rooms of bars and restaurants and put out front. During the 1930s locals constituted the vast majority of players; tourism showed little growth. If one looks carefully at the circumstances surrounding legalization of gambling, it is clear that no one contemplated the immense social and economic issues that would consume future state leaders. With no precedent to guide them, how could they?

Within two decades it had become apparent that Nevada had found a unique solution to its economic plight. With the end of the Great Depression, casino gambling developed into an economic dynamo that even the most optimistic booster could not have anticipated. By the early 1950s the once small and dusty railroad town of Las Vegas had entered a period of economic expansion that has not yet slowed. With a population of only 8,400 on the eve of the Second World War, Las Vegas grew to more than 125,000 residents by mid-century. When New York City mobster Benjamin "Bugsy" Siegel opened the Flamingo in 1947 on the two-lane highway heading south of town toward Los Angeles, he set in motion the building of the famous Las Vegas Strip. Within a few years the Flamingo was joined by increasingly larger and more opulent hotel-casinos—the Thunderbird (1948), Desert Inn (1950), Sands and Sahara (1952), and the Dunes, Stardust, Riviera, and an expanded New Frontier (1955).

The opening of Caesar's Palace in 1966 capped off an era of frenetic growth along the Strip, one that was accompanied by a substantial growth of gaming in downtown Las Vegas where such popular clubs as Benny Binion's Horseshoe Club, the Fremont, and the Golden Nugget flourished. Las Vegas underwent a period of consolidation and reform during the 1970s that featured intensification of state gaming controls and the introduction of corporate ownership of casinos. In the early 1980s a new generation of gambling visionaries, led by the hard-charging, charismatic Steve Wynn, produced a period of explosive growth that included such spectacular mega-resorts as the Mirage, Luxor, Excalibur, New York New York, MGM, and Bellagio. By the time Clark County enters the 21st century, its population will have reached 1,200,000.

The stunning transformation of Las Vegas into the world's entertainment-gaming capital dominated the second half of the twentieth-century Nevada history. In the process, "the city that never sleeps" has become one of the world's most famous places, its unique life style the subject of intensive examination by scholars, journalists, and the otherwise curious. When *Look* magazine called Las Vegas "Wild, Wooly, and Wide-Open" in a widely read article in 1940 that focused attention upon 24-hour gambling and substantial evidence of widespread prostitution, local citizens were aghast. They took special offense at the sentence that proclaimed that in Las Vegas "sin is a civic virtue." As the years passed, however, Las Vegans came to recognize that its unique lifestyle was what attracted ever increasing numbers of visitors each year, and similar denunciations were paid little heed.

They also took special satisfaction that their city had outstripped its long-time rival to the north. Irrepressibly smug Reno had dominated the economic and political life of the Silver State from the earliest days of statehood, but that changed quickly after the Second World War. Reno continued to identify itself as "The Biggest Little City in the World," a quaint motto that was a legacy of the 1930s, and provided an ironic commentary upon its new status as "number two." Las Vegas had become, in the eyes of social scientists and social commentators, the prototype of an emerging new urban form of the post-industrial era. That fact first occurred to journalist-social commentator Tom Wolfe in the mid-sixties as he observed in wonder the new values emerging along the famous Strip. No longer a dusty backwater town, Las Vegas had become recognized as one of the most complex and intriguing cities in the world. In 1994 *Time Magazine* proclaimed the nation's fastest growing metropolis the vanguard of emerging American cultural and social norms.

Although legalized gambling provided the primary impetus for the amazing Las Vegas story, it is important to understand that the city also benefitted from an enormous infusion of federal dollars. The completion of Boulder Dam in 1938 created Lake Mead, providing a source of water sufficient to support the desert city's growth. The establishment of Nellis Air Force Base to train many of the nation's fighter pilots during the Second World War, and the construction of the Basic Magnesium plant in nearby Henderson, contributed greatly to the city's growth. By 1943 Basic Magnesium employed 10,000 workers as it produced an important alloy that was used in the manufacture of lightweight military equipment and also was an important additive in powerful explosives. The Army Air Force also constructed bases at Fallon, Stead, Tonopah, and Wendover, each contributing to the state's economic revitalization.

During the early 1950s, the vast expanse of desert north of Las Vegas became the primary testing ground for nuclear weapons. Pentagon decision makers obviously assumed that Nevada's fragile desert environment had no other useful purpose, but Nevadans initially raised no significant opposition. In fact, they welcomed the construction of the Nevada Test Site. As the first above-ground tests were detonated, Las Vegans cheered even as windows shattered. The mushroom-shaped clouds that rose high over the desert sky eighty miles north of town were tangible signs of American strength in the Cold War. Las Vegas' patriotic citizens applauded as they sipped early morning cocktails at celebratory parties and felt the ground shake beneath their feet. They had no reason for fear because they had been assured by federal officials that the tests posed no health hazards. Nevada (and in particular nearby Las Vegas) thus became the beneficiary of huge—although unknown—amounts of federal money as America girded its nuclear loins for a potential showdown with the Soviet Union at the Nevada Test Site.

Nevada's humanists have long decried what they consider to be a lopsided image held by most Americans. A small army of novelists, poets, artists, anthropologists, environmentalists, photographers, and historians has sought to create a softer, sophisticated, more diverse, and (in their own eyes) more accurate image of the state. Their efforts have produced an impressive array of books and cultural artifacts, but their audience has often been restricted to fellow Nevadans, most of whom already perceived the many rich and diverse dimensions of Nevada. Several historians, most notably Wilbur Shepperson and Russell Elliott, have focused upon the complexity of the state's cultural heritage, and novelists Walter Van Tilburg Clark and Robert Laxalt succeeded in establishing themselves as writers of international stature who successfully used Nevada as a location to treat timeless issues related to the human condition. Distinguished environmental writers, from the pioneering John Muir to John McPhee and Ann Ronald, have written eloquently and persuasively about the power and grandeur of the Nevada wilderness that has eluded many casual observers unable to see beyond the bright lights of the casino districts or the vast bleak stretches of sagebrush and sand. This hidden Nevada contains a trove of cultural and natural treasures that the serious student of Nevada must not overlook.

As Nevada enters the twenty-first century, it confronts a wide spectrum of questions about its future. The distinguished Nevada historian James Hulse raised many hackles in 1989 when he revisited many old issues and coupled them with some emergent new ones to describe his native state as being "without a conscience." Many considered his critique overly harsh, but his major ideas cannot be easily dismissed. Although Hulse traced Nevada's problems to transcendent gambling interests, the industry's defenders noted that legalized gambling in one form or another had spread during the 1970s and 1980s to a majority of states, placing it well within the nation's economic and cultural mainstream. Thirty-seven states now sponsor lotteries, and nine have accepted some form of casino gambling, including such tradition-bound states as Minnesota, Indiana, and Iowa.

It is truly ironic that most of the major issues confronting contemporary Nevada revolve around the question of how it will manage its rapid growth. In 1900 Nevada confronted just the opposite dilemma—a crippling lack of growth, exacerbated by a shrinking population and characterized by a dearth of economic opportunities. Now Nevadans contemplate how to protect the state's fragile desert environment in the face of explosive urban growth, how to absorb continuing heavy immigration (including many new residents who do not speak English), and how to maintain essential public services for the nation's fastest-growing population.

Many complex problems confront state leaders, from funding a burgeoning educational system to dealing with very high rates of social pathologies that social scientists attribute to its dominant gaming culture: crime, suicide, alcohol and drug abuse, teen pregnancy, divorce, school drop-outs, low rates of college attendance, and mental illness. If the past is any indication, Nevada may very well tackle these problems with unconventional solutions that grow out of its unique, ironic heritage of being an economically conservative but socially liberal state. It would be surprising, even disappointing, if Nevada did not continue its role as a maverick state, resolutely attacking its problems with solutions that push the outer edge of political and social convention.

"First Meeting of Piutes and Whites"
(1883)

Sarah Winnemucca

Sarah Winnemucca was born "somewhere near 1844," the daughter of a leader of the Piute Tribe that had lived for centuries in north-central Nevada. As an adult she became an outspoken leader of the Piutes, and devoted much of her adult life to seeking assistance for her people, giving more than 400 speeches in Europe and the United States. Her book, from which this selection was taken, first appeared in 1883. After the death of her husband, Sarah Winnemucca Hopkins moved to Montana, where she died of tuberculosis in 1891.

I was born somewhere near 1844, but am not sure of the precise time. I was a very small child when the first white people came into our country. They came like a lion, yes, like a roaring lion, and have continued so ever since, and I have never forgotten their first coming. My people were scattered at that time over nearly all the territory now known as Nevada. My grandfather was chief of the entire Piute nation, and was camped near Humboldt Lake, with a small portion of his tribe, when a party traveling eastward from California was seen coming. When the news was brought to my grandfather, he asked what they looked like? When told that they had hair on their faces, and were white, he jumped up and clasped his hands together, and cried aloud, —

"My white brothers—my long-looked for white brothers have come at last!"

He immediately gathered some of his leading men, and went to the place where the party had gone into camp. Arriving near them, he was commanded to halt in a manner that was readily understood without an interpreter. Grandpa at once made signs of friendship by throwing down his robe and throwing up his arms to show them he had no weapons; but in vain,—they kept him at a distance. He knew not what to do. He had expected so much pleasure in welcoming his white brothers to the best in the land, that after looking at them sorrowfully for a little while, he came away quite unhappy. But he would not give them up so easily. He took some of his most trustworthy men and followed them day after day, camping near them at night, and traveling in sight of them by day, hoping in this way to gain their confidence. But he was disappointed, poor dear old soul!

I can imagine his feelings, for I have drank deeply from the same cup. When I think of my past life, and the bitter trials I have endured, I can scarcely believe I live, and yet I do; and, with the help of Him who notes the sparrow's fall, I mean to fight for my down-trodden race while life lasts.

Seeing they would not trust him, my grandfather left them, saying, "Perhaps they will come again next year." Then he summoned his whole people, and told them this tradition:—

"In the beginning of the world there were only four, two girls and two boys. Our forefather and mother were only two, and we are their children. You all know that a great while ago there was a happy family in this world. One girl and one boy were dark and the others were white. For a time they got along together without quarreling, but soon they disagreed, and there was trouble. They were cross to one another and fought, and our parents were very much grieved. They prayed that their children might learn better, but it did not do any good; and afterwards the whole household was made so unhappy that the father and mother saw that they must separate their children; and then our father took the dark boy and girl, and the white boy and girl, and asked them, 'Why are you so cruel to each other?' They hung down their heads, and would not speak. They were ashamed. He said to them, 'Have I not been kind to you all, and given you everything your hearts wished for? You do not have to hunt and kill your own game to live upon. You see, my dear children, I have power to call whatsoever kind of game we want to eat; and I also have the power to separate my dear children, if they are not good to each other.' So he separated his children by a word. He said, 'Depart from each other, you cruel children—go across the mighty ocean and do not seek each other's lives.'

"So the light girl and boy disappeared by that one word, and their parents saw them no more, and they were grieved, although they knew their children were happy. And by-and-by the dark children grew into a large nation; and we believe it is the one we belong to, and that the nation that sprung from the white children will some time send some one to meet us and heal all the old trouble. Now, the white people we saw a few days ago must certainly be our white brothers, and I want to welcome them. I want to love them as I love all of you. But they would not let me; they were afraid. But they will come again, and I want you one and all to promise that, should I not live to welcome them myself, you will not hurt a hair on their heads, but welcome them as I tried to do."

How good of him to try and heal the wound, and how vain were his efforts! My people had never seen a white man, and yet they existed, and were a strong race. The people promised as he wished, and they all went back to their work.

The next year came a great emigration, and camped near Humboldt Lake. The name of the man in charge of the trains was Captain Johnson, and they stayed three days to rest their horses, as they had a long journey before them without water. During their stay my grandfather and some of his people called upon them, and they all shook hands, and when our white brothers were going away they gave my grandfather a white tin plate. Oh, what a time they had over that beautiful gift,—it was so bright! They say that after they left my grandfather called for all his people to come together, and he then showed them the beautiful gift which he had received from his white brothers. Everybody was so pleased; nothing like it was ever seen in our country before. My grandfather thought so much of it that he bored holes in it and fastened it on his head, and wore it as his hat. He held it in as much admiration as my white sisters hold their diamond rings or a sealskin jacket. So that winter they talked of nothing but their white brothers. The following spring there came great news down the Humboldt River, saying that there were some more of the white brothers coming, and there was something among them that was burning all in a blaze. My grandfather asked them what it was like. They told him it looked like a man; it had legs and hands and a head, but the head had quit burning, and it was left quite black. There was the greatest excitement among my people everywhere about the men in a blazing fire. They were excited because they did not know there were any people in the world but the two,—that is, the Indians and the whites; they thought that was all of us in the beginning of the world, and, of course, we did not know where the others had come from, and we don't know yet. Ha! Ha! oh, what a laughable thing that was! It was two negroes wearing red shirts!

The third year more emigrants came, and that summer Captain Fremont, who is now General Fremont.

My grandfather met him, and they were soon friends. They met just where the railroad crosses Truckee River, now called Wadsworth, Nevada. Captain Fremont gave my grandfather the name of Captain Truckee, and he also called the river after him. Truckee is an Indian word, it means *all right*, or *very well*. A party of twelve of my people went to California with Captain Fremont. I do not know just how long they were gone.

During the time my grandfather was away in California, where he staid till after the Mexican war, there was a girl-baby born in our family. I can just remember it. It must have been in spring, because everything was green. I was away playing with some other children when my mother called me to come to her. So I ran to her. She then asked me to sit down, which I did. She then handed me some beautiful beads, and asked me if I would like to buy something with them. I said:—

"Yes, mother, —some pine nuts."

My mother said:—

"Would you like something else you can love and play with? Would you like to have a little sister?" I said,—

"Yes, dear mother, a little, little sister; not like my sister Mary, for she won't let me play with her. She leaves me and goes with big girls to play;" and then my mother wanted to know if I would give my pretty beads for the little sister.

Just then the baby let out such a cry it frightened me; and I jumped up and cried so that my mother took me in her arms and said it was a little sister for me, and not to be afraid. This is all I can remember about it.

When my grandfather want to California he helped Captain Fremont fight the Mexicans. When he came back he told the people what a beautiful country California was. Only eleven returned home, one having died on the way back.

They spoke to their people in the English language, which was very strange to them all.

Captain Truckee, my grandfather, was very proud of it, indeed. They all brought guns with them. My grandfather would sit down with us for hours, and would say over and over again, "Goodee gun, goodee, goodee gun, heap shoot." They also brought some of the soldiers' clothes with all their brass buttons, and my people were very much astonished to see the clothes, and all that time they were peaceable toward their white brothers. They had learned to love them, and they hoped more of them would come. Then my people were less barbarous than they are nowadays.

That same fall, after my grandfather came home, he told my father to take charge of his people and hold the tribe, as he was going back to California with as many of his people as he could get to go with him. So my father took his place as Chief of the Piutes, and had it as long as he lived. Then my grandfather started back to California again with about thirty families. That same fall, very late, the emigrants kept coming. It was this time that our white brothers first came amongst us. They could not get over the mountains, so they had to live with us. It was on Carson River, where the great Carson City stands now. You call my people bloodseeking. My people did not seek to kill them, nor did they steal their horses,— no, no, far from it. During the winter my people helped them. They gave them such as they had to eat. They did not hold out their hands and say:—

"You can't have anything to eat unless you pay me." No, —no such word was used by us savages at that time; and the persons I am speaking of are living yet; they could speak for us if they choose to do so.

The following spring, before my grandfather returned home, there was a great excitement among my people on account of fearful news coming from different tribes, that the people whom they called their white brothers were killing everybody that came in their way, and all the Indian tribes had gone into the mountains to save their lives. So my father told all his people to go into the mountains and hunt and lay up food for the coming winter. Then we all went into the mountains. There was a fearful story they told us children. Our mothers told us that the whites were killing everybody and eating them. So we were all afraid of them. Every dust that we could see blowing in the valleys we would say it was the white people. In the late fall my father told his people to go to the rivers and fish, and we all went to Humboldt River, and the women went to work gathering wild seed, which they grind between the rocks. The stones are round, big enough to hold in the hands. The women did this when they got back, and when they had gathered all they could they put it in one place and covered it with grass, and then over the grass mud. After it is covered it looks like an Indian wigwam.

Oh, what a fright we all got one morning to hear some white people were coming. Each one ran as best they could. My poor mother was left with my little sister and me. Oh, I never can forget it. My poor mother was carrying my little sister on her back, and trying to make me run; but I was so frightened I could not move my feet, and while my poor mother was trying to get me along my aunt overtook us, and she said to my mother: "Let us bury our girls, or we shall all be killed and eaten up." So they went to work and buried us, and told us if we heard any noise not to cry out, for if we did they would surely kill us and eat us. So our mothers buried me and my cousin, planted sage bushes over our faces to keep the sun from burning them, and there we were left all day.

Oh, can any one imagine my feelings *buried alive*, thinking every minute that I was to be unburied and eaten up by the people that my grandfather loved so much? With my heart throbbing, and not daring to breathe, we lay there all day. It seemed that the night would never come. Thanks be to God! The night came at last. Oh, how I cried and said: "Oh, father, have you forgotten me? Are you never coming for me?" I cried so I thought my very heartstrings would break.

At last we heard some whispering. We did not dare to whisper to each other, so we lay still. I could hear their footsteps coming nearer and nearer. I thought my heart was coming right out of my mouth. Then I heard my mother say, "'T is right here!" Oh, can any one in this world ever imagine what were my feelings when I was dug up by my poor mother and father? My cousin and I were once more happy in our mothers' and fathers' care, and we were taken to where all the rest were.

I was once buried alive; but my second burial shall be for ever, where no father or mother will come and dig me up. It shall not be with throbbing heart that I shall listen for coming footsteps. I shall be in the sweet rest of peace,—I, the chieftain's weary daughter.

Well, while we were in the mountains hiding, the people that my grandfather called our white brothers came along to where our winter supplies were. They set everything we had left on fire. It was a fearful sight. It was all we had for the winter, and it was all burnt during that night. My father took some of his men during the night to try and save some of it, but they could not; it had burnt down before they got there.

These were the last white men that came along that fall. My people talked fearfully that winter about those they called our white brothers. My people said they had something like awful thunder and lightning, and with that they killed everything that came in their way.

This whole band of white people perished in the mountains, for it was too late to cross them. We could have saved them, only my people were afraid of them. We never knew who they were, or where they came from. So, poor things, they must have suffered fearfully, for they all starved there. The snow was too deep.

Early in the following spring, my father told all his people to go to the mountains, for there would be a great emigration that summer. He told them he had had a wonderful dream, and wanted to tell them all about it.

He said, "Within ten days come together at the sink of Carson, and I will tell you my dream."

The sub-chiefs went everywhere to tell their people what my father had told them to say; and when the time came we all went to the sink of Carson.

Just about noon, while we were on the way, a great many of our men came to meet us, all on their horses. Oh, what a beautiful song they sang for my father as they came near us! We passed them, and they followed us, and as we came near to the encampment, every man, woman, and child were out looking for us. They had a place all ready for us. Oh, how happy everybody was! One could hear laughter everywhere, and songs were sung by happy women and children.

My father stood up and told his people to be merry and happy for five days. It is a rule among our people always to have five days to settle anything. My father told them to dance at night, and that the men should hunt rabbits and fish, and some were to have games of football, or any kind of sport or playthings they wished, and the women could do the same, as they had nothing else to do. My people were so happy during the five days,—the women ran races, and the men ran races on foot and on horses.

My father got up very early one morning, and told his people the time had come,—that we could no longer be happy as of old, as the white people we called our brothers had brought a great trouble and sorrow among us already. He went on and said,—

"These white people must be a great nation, as they have houses that move. It is wonderful to see them move along. I fear we will suffer greatly by their coming to our country; they come for no good to us, although my father said they were our brothers, but they do not seem to think we are like them. What do you all think about it? Maybe I am wrong. My dear children, there is something telling me that I am not wrong, because I am sure they have minds like us, and think as we do; and I know that they were doing wrong when they set fire to our winter supplies. They surely knew it was our food."

And this was the first wrong done to us by our white brothers.

Now comes the end of our merrymaking.

Then my father told his people his fearful dream, as he called it. He said,—

"I dreamt this same thing three nights,—the very same. I saw the greatest emigration that has yet been through our country. I looked North and South and East and West, and saw nothing but dust, and I heard a great weeping. I saw women crying, and I also saw my men shot down by the white people. They were killing my people with something that made a great noise like thunder and lightning, and I saw the blood streaming from the mouths of my men that lay all around me. I saw it as if it was real. Oh, my dear children! You may all think it is only a dream,—nevertheless, I feel that it will come to pass. And to avoid bloodshed, we must all go to the mountains during the summer, or till my father comes back from California. He will then tell us what to do. Let us keep away from the emigrant roads and stay in the mountains all summer. There are to be a great many pine-nuts this summer, and we can lay up great supplies for the coming winter, and if the emigrants don't come too early, we can take a run down and fish for a month, and lay up dried fish. I know we can dry a great many in a month, and young men can go into the valleys on hunting excursions, and kill as many rabbits as they can. In that way we can live in the mountains all summer and all winter too."

So ended my father's dream. During that day one could see old women getting together talking over what they had heard my father say. "They said,—

"It is true what our great chief has said, for it was shown to him by a higher power. It is not a dream. Oh, it surely will come to pass. We shall no longer be a happy people, as we now are; we shall no longer go here and there as of old; we shall no longer build our big fires as a signal to our friends, for we shall always be afraid of being seen by those bad people."

"Surely they don't eat people?"

"Yes, they do eat people, because they ate each other up in the mountains last winter."

This was the talk among the old women during the day.

"Oh, how grieved we are! Oh, where will it end?"

That evening one of our doctors called for a council, and all the men gathered together in the council-tent to hear what their medicine man had to say, for we all believe our doctor is greater than any human being living. We do not call him a medicine man because he gives medicine to the sick, as your doctors do. Our medicine man cures the sick by the laying on of hands, and we have doctresses as well as doctors. We believe that our doctors can communicate with holy spirits from heaven. We call heaven the Spirit Land.

Well, when all the men get together, of course there must be smoking the first thing. After the pipe has passed round five times to the right, it stops, and then he tells them to sing five songs. He is the leader in the song-singing. He sings heavenly songs, and he says he is singing with the angels. It is hard to describe these songs. They are all different, and he says the angels sing them to him.

Our doctors never sing war-songs, except at a war dance, as they never go themselves on the warpath. While they were singing the last song, he said,—

"Now I am going into a trance. While I am in the trance you must smoke just as you did before; not a word must be spoken while I am in the trance."

About fifteen minutes after the smoking was over, he began to make a noise as if he was crying a great way off. The noise came nearer and nearer, until he breathed, and after he came to, he kept on crying. And then he prophesied, and told the people that my father's dream was true in one sense of the word,—that is, "Our people will not all die at the hands of our white brothers. They will kill a great many with their guns, but they will bring among us a fearful disease that will cause us to die by hundreds."

We all wept, for we believed this word came from heaven.

So ended our feast, and every family went to its own home in the pine-nut mountains, and remained there till the pine-nuts were ripe. They ripen about the last of June.

Late in that fall, there came news that my grandfather was on his way home. Then my father took a great many of his men and went to meet his father, and there came back a runner, saying, that all our people must come together. It was said that my grandfather was bringing bad news. All our people came to receive their chieftain; all the old and young men and their wives went to meet him. One evening there came a man, saying that all the women who had little children should go to a high mountain. They wanted them to go because they brought white men's guns, and they made such a fearful noise, it might even kill some of the little children. My grandfather had lost one of his men while he was away.

So all the women that had little children went. My mother was among the rest; and every time the guns were heard by us, the children would scream. I thought, for one that my heart would surely break. So some of the women went down from the mountain and told them not to shoot any more, or their children would die with fright. When our mothers brought us down to our homes the nearer we came to the camp, the more I cried,—

"Oh, mother, mother, don't take us there!" I fought my mother,—I bit her. Then my father came, and took me in his arms and carried me to the camp. I put my head in his bosom, and would not look up for a long time. I heard my grandfather say,—

"So the young lady is ashamed because her sweetheart has come to see her. Come, dearest, that won't do after I have had such a hard time to come to see my sweetheart, that she should be ashamed to look at me."

Then he called my two brothers to him, and said to them, "Are you glad to see me?" And my brothers both told him that they were glad to see him. Then my grandfather said to them,—

"See that young lady; she does not love her sweetheart any more, does she? Well, I shall not live if she does not come and tell me she loves me. I shall take that gun, and I shall kill myself."

That made me worse than ever, and I screamed and cried so hard that my mother had to take me away. So they kept weeping for the little one three or four days. I did not make up with my grandfather for a long time. He sat day after day, and night after night, telling his people about his white brothers. He told them that the whites were really their brothers, that they were very kind to everybody, especially to children; that they were always ready to give something to children. He told them what beautiful things their white brothers had,—what beautiful clothes they wore, and about the big houses that go on the mighty ocean, and travel faster than any horse in the world. His people asked him how big they were. "Well, as big as that hill you see there, and as high as the mountain over us."

"Oh, that is not possible,—it would sink, surely."

"It is every word truth, and that is nothing to what I am going to tell you. Our white brothers are a mighty nation, and have more wonderful things than that. They have a gun that can shoot a ball bigger than my head, that can go as far off as that mountain you see over there."

The mountain he spoke of at that time was about twenty miles across from where we were. People opened their eyes when my grandfather told of the many battles they had with the Mexicans, and about their killing so many of the Mexicans, and taking their big city away from them, and how mighty they were. These wonderful things were talked about all winter long. The funniest thing was that he would sing some of the soldier's roll-calls, and the air to the Star-spangled Banner, which everybody learned during the winter.

He then showed us a more wonderful thing than all the others that he had brought. It was a paper, which he said could talk to him. He took it out and he would talk to it, and talk with it. He said, "This can talk to all our white brothers, and our white sisters, and their children. Our white brothers are beautiful, and our white sisters are beautiful, and their children are beautiful! He also said the paper can travel like the wind, and it can go and talk with their fathers and brothers and sisters, and come back to tell what they are doing, and whether they are well or sick."

After my grandfather told us this, our doctors and doctresses said,—

"If they can do this wonderful thing, they are not truly human, but pure spirits. None but heavenly spirits can do such wonderful things. We can communicate with the spirits, yet we cannot do wonderful things like them. Oh, our great chieftain, we are afraid your white brothers will yet make your people's hearts bleed. You see if they don't; for we can see it. Their blood is all around us, and the dead are lying all about us, and we cannot escape it. It will come. Then you will say our doctors and doctresses did not know. Dance, sing, play, it will do no good; we cannot drive it away. They have already done the mischief, while you were away."

But this did not go far with my grandfather. He kept talking to his people about the good white people, and told them all to get ready to go with him to California the following spring.

Very late that fall, my grandfather and my father and a great many more went down to the Humboldt River to fish. They brought back a great many fish, which we were very glad to get; for none of our people had been down to fish the whole summer.

When they came back, they brought us more news. They said there were some white people living at the Humboldt sink. They were the first ones my father had seen face to face. He said they were not like "humans." They were more like owls than any thing else. They had hair on their faces, and had white eyes, and looked beautiful.

I tell you we children had to be very good, indeed, during the winter; for we were told that if we were not good they would come and eat us up. We remained there all winter; the next spring the emigrants came as usual, and my father and grandfather and uncles, and many more went down on the Humboldt River on fishing excursions. While they were thus fishing, their white brothers came upon them and fired on them, and killed one of my uncles, and wounded another. Nine more were wounded, and five died afterwards. My other uncle got well again, and is living yet. Oh, that was a fearful thing, indeed!

After all these things had happened, my grandfather still stood up for his white brothers.

Our people had council after council, to get my grandfather to give his consent that they should go and kill those white men who were at the sink of Humboldt. No; they could do nothing of the kind while he lived. He told his people that his word was more to him than his son's life, or any one else's life either.

"Dear children," he said, "think of your own words to me;—you promised. You want me to say to you, Go and kill those that are at the sink of Humboldt. After your promise, how dare you to ask me to let your hearts be stained with the blood of those who are innocent of the deed that has been done to us by others? Is not my dear beloved son laid alongside of your dead, and you say I stand up for their lives. Yes, it is very hard, indeed; but, nevertheless, I know and you know that those men who live at the sink are not the ones that killed our men."

While my grandfather was talking, he wept, and men, women, and children, were all weeping. One could hardly hear him talking.

After he was through talking, came the saddest part. The widow of my uncle who was killed, and my mother and father all had long hair. They cut off their hair, and also cut long gashes in their arms and legs, and they were all bleeding as if they would die with the loss of blood. This continued for several days, for this is the way we mourn for our dead. When the woman's husband dies, she is first to cut off her hair, and then she braids it and puts it across his breast; then his mother and sisters, his father and brothers and all his kinsfolk cut their hair. The widow is to remain unmarried until her hair is the same length as before, and her face is not to be washed all that time, and she is to use no kind of paint, or to make any merriment with other women until the day is set for her to do so by her father-in-law, or if she has no father-in-law, by her mother-in-law, and then she is at liberty to go where she pleases. The widower is at liberty when his wife dies; but he mourns for her in the same way, by cutting his hair off.

It was late that fall when my grandfather prevailed with his people to go with him to California. It was this time that my mother accompanied him. Everything had been got ready to start on our journey. My dear father was to be left behind. How my poor mother begged to stay with her husband! But my grandfather told her that she could come back in the spring to see her husband; so we started for California, leaving my poor papa behind. All my kinsfolk went with us but one aunt and her children.

The first night found us camped at the sink of Carson, and the second night we camped on Carson River. The third day, as we were traveling along the river, some of our men who were ahead, came back and said there were some of our white brothers' houses ahead of us. So my grandfather told us all to stop where we were while he went to see them. He was not gone long, and when he came back he brought some hard bread which they gave him. He told us that was their food, and he gave us all some to taste. That was the first I ever tasted.

Then my grandfather once more told his people that his paper talked for him, and he said,—

"Just as long as I live and have that paper which my white brothers' great chieftain has given me, I shall stand by them, come what will." He held the paper up towards heaven and kissed it, as if it was really a person. "Oh, if I should lose this," he said, "we shall all be lost. So, children, get your horses ready, and we will go on, and we will camp with them tonight, or by them, for I have a sweetheart along who is dying for fear of my white brothers." He meant me; for I was always crying and hiding under somebody's robes, for we had no blankets then.

Well, we went on; but we did not camp with them, because my poor mother and brothers and sisters told my grandfather that I was sick with crying for fright, and for him not to camp too close to them. The women were speaking two words for themselves and one for me, for they were just as afraid as I was. I had seen my brother Natchez crying when the men came back, and said there were white men ahead of us. So my grandfather did as my mother wished him to do, and we went on by them; but I did not know it, as I had my head covered while we were passing their camp. I was riding behind my older brother, and we went on and camped quite a long way from them that night.

So we traveled on to California, but did not see any more of our white brothers till we got to the head of Carson River, about fifteen miles above where great Carson City now stands.

"Now give me the baby." It was my baby-sister that grandpa took from my mother, and I peeped from under my mother's fur, and I saw some one take my little sister. Then I cried out,—

"Oh, my sister! Don't let them take her away."

And once more my poor grandfather told his people that his white brothers and sisters were very kind to children. I stopped crying, and looked at them again. Then I saw them give my brother and sister something white. My mother asked her father what it was, and he said it was *Pe-har-be*, which means sugar. Just then one of the women came to my mother with some in her hand, and grandpa said:—

"Take it, my child."

Then I held out my hand without looking. That was the first gift I ever got from a white person, which made my heart very glad.

When they went away, my grandfather called me to him, and said I must not be afraid of the white people, for they are very good. I told him that they looked so very bad I could not help it. . . .

from *Roughing It*
(1871)

Mark Twain
(Samuel Clemens)

When his older brother Orion was named Secretary to the Territorial Governor of Nevada, young Samuel Clemens made a lengthy journey by coach from Missouri to Carson City. Clemens' wry if often exaggerated description of this marvelous adventure, which eventually took him to California and Hawaii, was published in 1871. He spent three years (1861–64) living in northern Nevada. After living in Carson City for a brief time, he became a mill hand and timber claim owner in the Humboldt and Esmeralda Mining Districts, before accepting the position of reporter for the Virginia City Territorial Enterprise, one of the most influential western newspapers of this era. His writings reflected his willingness to attempt satire and burlesque as well as serious commentary. Selections of his observations of territorial Nevada—the land, the politicians, the miners on the Comstock—have been excerpted from his early classic, Roughing It.

My brother had just been appointed Secretary of Nevada Territory—an office of such majesty that it concentrated in itself the duties and dignities of Treasurer, Comptroller, Secretary of State, and Acting Governor in the Governor's absence. A salary of eighteen hundred dollars a year and the title of "Mr. Secretary," gave to the great position an air of wild and imposing grandeur. I was young and ignorant, and I envied my brother. I coveted his distinction and his financial splendor, but particularly and especially the long, strange journey he was going to make, and the curious new world he was going to explore. He was going to travel! I never had been away from home, and that word "travel" had a seductive charm for me. Pretty soon he would be hundreds and hundreds of miles away on the great plains and deserts, and among the mountains of the Far West, and would see buffaloes and Indians, and prairie-dogs, and antelopes, and have all kinds of adventures, and maybe get hanged or scalped, and have ever such a fine time, and write home and tell us all about it, and be a hero. And he would see the gold-mines and the silver-mines, and maybe go about of an afternoon when his work was done, and pick up two or three pailfuls of shining slugs and nuggets of gold and silver on the hillside. And by and by he would become very rich, and return home by sea, and be able to talk as calmly about San Francisco and the ocean and "the isthmus" as if it was nothing of any consequence to have seen those marvels face to face. What I suffered in contemplating his happiness, pen cannot describe. And so, when he offered me, in cold blood, the sublime position of private secretary under him, it appeared to me that the heavens and the earth passed away, and the firmament was rolled together as a scroll! I had nothing more to desire. My contentment was complete. At the end of an hour or two I was ready for the journey. Not much packing up was necessary, because we were going in the overland stage from the Missouri frontier to Nevada, and passengers were only allowed a small quantity of baggage apiece. There was no Pacific railroad in those fine times of ten or twelve years ago—not a single rail of it.

I only proposed to stay in Nevada three months—I had no thought of staying longer than that. I meant to see all I could that was new and strange, and then hurry home to business. I little thought that I would not see the end of that three-month pleasure excursion for six or seven uncommonly long years!

I dreamed all night about Indians, deserts, and silver bars, and in due time, next day, we took shipping at the St. Louis wharf on board a steamboat bound up the Missouri River. . . .

We were approaching the end of our long journey. It was the morning of the twentieth day. At noon we would reach Carson City, the capital of Nevada Territory. We were not glad, but sorry. It had been a fine pleasure trip; we had fed fat on wonders every day; we were now well accustomed to stage life, and very fond of it; so the idea of coming to a standstill and settling down to a hum-drum existence in a village was not agreeable, but on the contrary depressing.

Visibly our new home was a desert, walled in by barren, snow-clad mountains. There was not a tree in sight. There was no vegetation but the endless sagebrush and greasewood. All nature was gray with it. We were plowing through great deeps of powdery alkali dust that rose in thick clouds and floated across the plain like smoke from a burning house. We were coated with it like millers; so were the coach, the mules, the mail-bags, the driver—we and the sagebrush and the other scenery were all one monotonous color. Long trains of freight-wagons in the distance enveloped in ascending masses of dust suggested pictures of prairies on fire. These teams and their masters were the only life we saw. Otherwise we moved in the midst of solitude, silence, and desolation. Every twenty steps we passed the skeleton of some dead beast of burden, with its dust-coated skin stretched tightly over its empty ribs. Frequently a solemn raven sat upon the skull or the hips and contemplated the passing coach with meditative serenity.

By and by Carson City was pointed out to us. It nestled in the edge of a great plain and was a sufficient number of miles away to look like an assemblage of mere white spots in the shadow of a grim range of mountains overlooking it, whose summits seemed lifted clear out of companionship and consciousness of earthly things.

We arrived, disembarked, and the stage went on. It was a "wooden" town; its population two thousand souls. The main street consisted of four or five blocks of little white frame stores which were too high to sit down on, but not too high for various other purposes; in fact, hardly high enough. They were packed close together, side by side, as if room were scarce in that mighty plain. The sidewalk was of boards that were more or less loose and inclined to rattle when walked upon. In the middle of the town, opposite the stores, was the "plaza," which is native to all towns beyond the Rocky Mountains—a large, un-fenced, level vacancy, with a liberty pole in it, and very useful as a place for public auctions, horse trades, and mass-meetings, and likewise for teamsters to camp in. Two other sides of the plaza were faced by stores, offices, and stables. The rest of Carson City was pretty scattering.

We were introduced to several citizens, at the stage-office and on the way up to the Governor's from the hotel—among others, to a Mr. Harris, who was on horseback; he began to say something, but interrupted himself with the remark:

"I'll have to get you to excuse me a minute; yonder is the witness that swore I helped to rob the California coach—a piece of impertinent intermeddling, sir, for I am not even ac-quainted with the man."

Then he rode over and began to rebuke the stranger with a six-shooter, and the stranger began to explain with another. When the pistols were emptied, the stranger resumed his work (mending a whiplash), and Mr. Harris rode by with a polite nod, homeward bound, with a bullet through one of his lungs, and several through his hips; and from them issued little rivulets of blood that coursed down the horse's sides and made the animal look quite picturesque. I never saw Harris shoot a man after that but it recalled to mind that first day in Carson.

This was all we saw that day, for it was two o'clock, now, and according to custom the daily "Washoe Zephyr" set in; a soaring dust-drift about the size of the United States set up edgewise came with it, and the capital of Nevada Territory disappeared from view. Still, there were sights to be seen which were not wholly uninteresting to newcomers; for the vast dust-cloud was thickly freckled with things strange to the upper air—things living and dead, that flitted hither and thither, going and coming, appearing and disappearing among the rolling billows of dust—hats, chickens, and parasols sailing in the remote heavens; blankets, tin signs, sage-brush, and shingles a shade lower; door-mats and buffalo-robes lower still; shovels and coal-scuttles on the next grade; glass doors, cats, and little children on the next; disrupted lumber yards, light buggies, and wheelbarrows on the next; and down only thirty or forty feet above ground was a scurrying storm of emigrating roofs and vacant lots.

It was something to see that much. I could have seen more, if I could have kept the dust out of my eyes.

But, seriously, a Washoe wind is by no means a trifling matter. It blows flimsy houses down, lifts shingle roofs occasionally, rolls up tin ones like sheet music, now and then blows a stage-coach over and spills the passengers; and tradition says the reason there are so many bald people there is, that the wind blows the hair off their heads while they are looking skyward after their hats. Carson streets seldom look inactive on summer afternoons, because there are so many citizens skipping around their escaping hats, like chambermaids trying to head off a spider.

The "Washoe Zephyr" (Washoe is a pet nickname for Nevada) is a peculiarly Scriptural wind, in that no man knoweth "whence it cometh." That is to say, where it *originates*. It comes right over the mountains from the West, but when one crosses the ridge he does not find any of it on the other side! It probably is manufactured on the mountaintop for the occasion, and starts from there. It is a pretty regular wind, in the summertime. Its office-hours are from two in the afternoon till two the next morning; and anybody venturing abroad during those twelve hours needs to allow for the wind or he will bring up a mile or two to leeward of the point he is aiming at. And yet the first complaint a Washoe visitor to San Francisco makes, is that the sea-winds blow so, there! There is a good deal of human nature in that.

We found the state palace of the Governor of Nevada Territory to consist of a white frame one story house with two small rooms in it and a stanchion-supported shed in front—for grandeur—it compelled the respect of the citizen and inspired the Indians with awe. The newly arrived Chief and Associate Justices of the territory, and other machinery of the government, were domiciled with less splendor. They were boarding around privately, and had their offices in their bedrooms. . . .

By and by I was smitten with the silver fever. "Prospecting parties" were leaving for the mountains every day, and discovering and taking possession of rich silver-bearing lodes and ledges of quartz. Plainly this was the road to fortune. The great "Gould and Curry" mine was held at three or four hundred dollars a foot when we arrived; but in two months it had sprung up to eight hundred. The "Ophir" had been worth only a mere trifle, a year gone by, and now it was selling at nearly *four thousand dollars a foot!* Not a mine could be named that had not experienced an astonishing advance in value within a short time. Everybody was talking about these marvels. Go where you would, you heard nothing else, from morning till far into the night. Tom So-and-So had sold out of the "Amanda Smith" for $40,000—hadn't a cent when he "took up" the ledge six months ago. John Jones had sold half his interest in the "Bald Eagle and Mary Ann" for $65,000, gold coin, and gone to the States for his family. The widow Brewster had "struck it rich" in the "Golden Fleece" and sold ten feet for $18,000—hadn't money enough to buy a crepe bonnet when Sing-Sing Tommy killed her husband at Baldy Johnson's wake last spring. The "Last Chance" had found a "clay casing" and knew they were "right on the ledge"—consequence, "feet" that went begging yesterday were worth a brick house apiece today, and seedy owners who could not get trusted for a drink at any bar in the country yesterday were roaring drunk on champagne today and had hosts of warm personal friends in a town where they had forgotten how to bow or shake hands from long-continued want of practice. Johnny Morgan, a common loafer, had gone to sleep in the gutter and waked up worth a hundred thousand dollars, in consequence of the decision in the "Lady Franklin and Rough and Ready" lawsuit. And so—day in and day out the talk pelted our ears and the excitement waxed hotter and hotter around us.

I would have been more or less than human if I had not gone mad like the rest. Cartloads of solid silver bricks, as large as pigs of lead, were arriving from the mills every day, and such sights as that gave substance to the wild talk about me. I succumbed and grew as frenzied as the craziest.

Every few days news would come of the discovery of a brand new mining region; immediately the papers would teem with accounts of its richness, and away the surplus population would scamper to take possession. By the time I was fairly inoculated with the disease, "Esmeralda" had just had a run and "Humboldt" was beginning to shriek for attention. "Humboldt! Humboldt!" was the new cry, and straightway Humboldt, the newest of the new, the richest of the rich, the most marvelous of the marvelous discoveries in silver-land, was occupying two columns of the public prints to "Esmeralda's" one. I was just on the point of starting to Esmeralda, but turned with the tide and got ready for Humboldt. That the reader may see what moved me, and what would as surely have moved him had he been there, I insert here one of the newspaper letters of the day. It and several other letters from the same calm hand were the main means of converting me. I shall not garble the extract, but put it in just as it appeared in the *Daily Territorial Enterprise*.

> But what about our mines? I shall be candid with you. I shall express an honest opinion, based upon a thorough examination. Humboldt County is the richest mineral region upon God's footstool. Each mountain range is gorged with the precious ores. Humboldt is the true Golconda.
>
> The other day an assay of mere *croppings* yielded exceeding *four thousand dollars to the ton*. A week or two ago an assay of just such surface developments made returns of *seven thousand* dollars to the ton. Our mountains are full of rambling prospectors. Each day and almost every hour reveals new and more startling evidences of the profuse and intensified wealth of our favored county. The metal is not silver alone. There are distinct ledges of auriferous ore. A late discovery plainly evinces cinnabar. The coarser metals are in gross abundance. Lately evidences of bituminous coal have been detected. My theory has ever been that coal is a ligneous formation. I told Col. Whitman, in times past, that the neighborhood of Dayton (Nevada) betrayed no present or previous manifestations of a ligneous foundation, and that hence I had no confidence in his lauded coal-mines. I repeated the same doctrine to the exultant coal-discoverers of Humboldt. I talked with my friend Captain Burch on the subject. My pyrhanism vanished upon his statement that in the very region referred to he had seen petrified trees of the length of two hundred feet. Then is the fact established that huge forests once cast their grim shadows over this remote section. I am firm in the coal faith. Have no fears of the mineral resources of Humboldt County. They are immense—incalculable.

Let me state one or two things which will help the reader to better comprehend certain items in the above. At this time, our near neighbor, Gold Hill, was the most successful silver-mining locality in Nevada. It was from there that more than half the daily shipments of silver bricks came. "Very rich" (and scarce) Gold Hill ore yielded from $100 to $400 to the ton; but the usual yield was only $20 to $40 per ton—that is to say, each hundred pounds of ore yielded from one dollar to two dollars. But the reader will perceive by the above extract, that in Humboldt from one-fourth to nearly half the mass was silver! That is to say, every one hundred pounds of the ore had from *two hundred* dollars up to about *three hundred and fifty* in it. Some days later this same correspondent wrote:

> I have spoken of the vast and almost fabulous wealth of this region—it is incredible. The intestines of our mountains are gorged with precious ore to plethora. I have said that nature has so shaped our mountains as to furnish most excellent facilities for the working of our mines. I have also told you that the country about here is pregnant

with the finest mill sites in the world. But what is the mining history of Humboldt? The Sheba mine is in the hands of energetic San Francisco capitalists. It would seem that the ore is combined with metals that render it difficult of reduction with our imperfect mountain machinery. The proprietors have combined the capital and labor hinted at in my exordium. They are toiling and probing. Their tunnel has reached the length of one hundred feet. From primal assays alone, coupled with the development of the mine and public confidence in the continuance of effort, the stock had reared itself to eight hundred dollars market value. I do not know that one ton of the ore has been converted into current metal. I do know that there are many lodes in this section that surpass the Sheba in primal assay value. Listen a moment to the calculations of the Sheba operators. They purpose transporting the ore concentrated to Europe. The conveyance from Star City (its locality) to Virginia City will cost seventy dollars per ton; from Virginia to San Francisco, forty dollars per ton; from thence to Liverpool, its destination, ten dollars per ton. Their idea is that its conglomerate metals will reimburse them their cost of original extraction, the price of transportation, and the expense of reduction, and that then a ton of the raw ore will net them twelve hundred dollars. The estimate may be extravagant. Cut it in twain, and the product is enormous, far transcending any previous developments of our racy territory.

A very common calculation is that many of our mines will yield five hundred dollars to the ton. Such fecundity throws the Gould & Curry, the Ophir and the Mexican, of your neighborhood, in the darkest shadow. I have given you the estimate of the value of a single developed mine. Its richness is indexed by its market valuation. The people of Humboldt County are *feet* crazy. As I write, our towns are near deserted. They look as languid as a consumptive girl. What has become of our sinewy and athletic fellow-citizens? They are coursing through ravines and over mountain-tops. Their tracks are visible in every direction. Occasionally a horseman will dash among us. His steed betrays hard usage. He alights before his adobe dwelling, hastily exchanges courtesies with his townsmen, hurries to an assay office and from thence to the District Recorder's. In the morning, having renewed his provisional supplies, he is off again on his wild and unbeaten route. Why, the fellow numbers already his feet by the thousands. He is the horse-leech. He has the craving stomach of the shark or anaconda. He would conquer metallic worlds.

This was enough. The instant we had finished reading the above article, four of us decided to go to Humboldt. We commenced getting ready at once. And we also commenced upbraiding ourselves for not deciding sooner—for we were in terror lest all the rich mines would be found and secured before we got there, and we might have to put up with ledges that would not yield more than two or three hundred dollars a ton, maybe. An hour before, I would have felt opulent if I had owned ten feet in a Gold Hill mine whose ore produced twenty-five dollars to the ton; now I was already annoyed at the prospect of having to put up with mines the poorest of which would be a marvel in Gold Hill.

Hurry, was the word! We wasted no time. Our party consisted of four persons—a blacksmith sixty years of age, two young lawyers, and myself. We bought a wagon and two miserable old horses. We put eighteen hundred pounds of provisions and mining-tools in the wagon and drove out of Carson on a chilly December afternoon. . . .

We were fifteen days making the trip—two hundred miles; thirteen, rather, for we lay by a couple of days, in one place, to let the horses rest. . . .

It was a hard, wearing, toilsome journey, but it had its bright side; for after each day was done and our wolfish hunger appeased with a hot supper of fried bacon, bread, molasses, and black coffee, the pipe-smoking, song-singing, and yarn-spinning around the evening campfire in the still solitudes of the desert was a happy, carefree sort of recreation that seemed the very summit and culmination of earthly luxury. It is a kind of life that has a potent charm for all men, whether city or country bred. We are descended from desert-lounging Arabs, and countless ages of growth toward perfect civilization have failed to root out of us the nomadic instinct. We all confess to a gratified thrill at the thought of "camping out."

Once we made twenty-five miles in a day, and once we made forty miles (through the Great American Desert), and ten miles beyond—fifty in all—in twenty-three hours, without halting to eat, drink, or rest. To stretch out and go to sleep, even on stony and frozen ground, after pushing a wagon and two horses fifty miles, is a delight so supreme that for the moment it almost seems cheap at the price. We camped two days in the neighborhood of the " Sink of the Humboldt." We tried to use the strong alkaline water of the Sink, but it would not answer. It was like drinking lye, and not weak lye, either. It left a taste in the mouth, bitter and every way execrable, and a burning in the stomach that was very uncomfortable. We put molasses in it, but that helped it very little; we added a pickle, yet the alkali was the prominent taste, and so it was unfit for drinking. The coffee we made of this water was the meanest compound man has yet invented. It was really viler to the taste than the unameliorated water itself. Mr. Ballou, being the architect and builder of the beverage, felt constrained to indorse and uphold it, and so drank half a cup, by little sips, making shift to praise it faintly the while, but faintly threw out the remainder, and said frankly it was "too technical for *him*."

But presently we found a spring of fresh water, convenient, and then, with nothing to mar our enjoyment, and no stragglers to interrupt it, we entered into our rest.

After leaving the Sink, we traveled along the Humboldt River a little way. People accustomed to the monster mile-wide Mississippi, grow accustomed to associating the term "river" with a high degree of watery grandeur. Consequently, such people feel rather disappointed when they stand on the shores of the Humboldt or the Carson and find that a "river" in Nevada is a sickly rivulet which is just the counterpart of the Erie canal in all respects save that the canal is twice as long and four times as deep. One of the pleasantest and most invigorating exercises one can contrive is to run and jump across the Humboldt River till he is overheated, and then drink it dry.

On the fifteenth day we completed our march of two hundred miles and entered Unionville, Humboldt County, in the midst of a driving snow- storm. Unionville consisted of eleven cabins and a liberty pole. Six of the cabins were strung along one side of a deep cañon, and the other five faced them. The rest of the landscape was made up of bleak mountain walls that rose so high into the sky from both sides of the cañon that the village was left, as it were, far down in the bottom of a crevice. It was always daylight on the mountain-tops a long time before the darkness lifted and revealed Unionville.

We built a small, rude cabin in the side of the crevice and roofed it with canvas, leaving a corner open to serve as a chimney, through which the cattle used to tumble occasionally, at night, and mash our furniture and interrupt our sleep. It was very cold weather and fuel was scarce. Indians brought brush and bushes several miles on their backs; and when we could catch a laden Indian it was well—and when we could not (which was the rule, not the exception), we shivered and bore it.

I confess, without shame, that I expected to find masses of silver lying all about the ground. I expected to see it glittering in the sun on the mountain summits. I said nothing about this, for some instinct told me that I might possibly have an exaggerated idea about it, and so if I betrayed my thought I might bring derision upon myself. Yet I was as perfectly satisfied in my own mind as I could be of anything, that I was going to gather up, in a day or two, or at furthest a week or two, silver enough to make me satisfactorily wealthy—and so my fancy was already busy with plans for spending this money. The first opportunity that offered, I sauntered carelessly away from the cabin, keeping an eye on the other boys, and stopping and contemplating the sky when they seemed to be observing me; but as soon as the coast was manifestly clear, I fled away as guiltily as a thief might have done and never halted till I was far beyond sight and call. Then I began my search with a feverish excitement that was brimful of expectation—almost of certainty. I crawled about the ground, seizing and examining bits of stone, blowing the dust from them or rubbing them on my clothes, and then peering at them with anxious hope. Presently I found a bright fragment and my heart bounded! I hid behind a boulder and polished it and scrutinized it with a nervous eagerness and a delight that was more pronounced than absolute certainty itself could have afforded. The more I examined the fragment the more I was convinced that I had found the door to fortune. I marked the spot and carried away my specimen. Up and down the rugged mountainside I searched, with always increasing interest and always augmenting gratitude that I had come to Humboldt and come in time. Of all the experiences of my life, this secret search among the hidden treasures of silver-land was the nearest to unmarred ecstasy. It was a delirious revel. By and by, in the bed of a shallow rivulet, I found a deposit of shining yellow scales, and my breath almost forsook me! A gold-mine, and in my simplicity I had been content with vulgar silver! I was so excited that I half believed my overwrought imagination was deceiving me. Then a fear came upon me that people might be observing me and would guess my secret. Moved by this thought, I made a circuit of the place, and ascended a knoll to reconnoiter. Solitude. No creature was near. Then I returned to my mine, fortifying myself against possible disappointment, but my fears were groundless—the shining scales were still there. I set about scooping them out, and for an hour I toiled down the windings of the stream and robbed its bed. But at last the descending sun warned me to give up the quest, and I turned homeward laden with wealth. As I walked along I could not help smiling at the thought of my being so excited over my fragment of silver when a nobler metal was almost under my nose. In this little time the former had so fallen in my estimation that once or twice I was on the point of throwing it away.

The boys were as hungry as usual, but I could eat nothing. Neither could I talk. I was full of dreams and far away. Their conversation interrupted the flow of my fancy somewhat, and annoyed me a little, too. I despised the sordid and commonplace things they talked about. But as they proceeded, it began to amuse me. It grew to be rare fun to hear them planning their poor little economies and sighing over possible privations and distresses when a gold-mine, all our own, lay within sight of the cabin, and I could point it out at any moment. Smothered hilarity began to oppress me, presently. It was hard to resist the impulse to burst out with exultation and reveal everything; but I did resist. I said within myself that I would filter the great news through my lips calmly and be serene as a summer morning while I watched its effect in their faces. I said:

"Where have you all been?"

"Prospecting."

"What did you find?"

"Nothing."

"Nothing? What do you think of the country?"

"Can't tell, yet," said Mr. Ballou, who was an old gold-miner, and had likewise had considerable experience among the silver-mines.

"Well, haven't you formed any sort of opinion?"

"Yes, a sort of a one. It's fair enough here, maybe, but overrated. Seven-thousand-dollar ledges are scarce, though. That Sheba may be rich enough, but we don't own it; and, besides, the rock is so full of base metals that all the science in the world can't work it. We'll not starve, here, but we'll not get rich, I'm afraid."

"So you think the prospect is pretty poor?"

"No name for it!"

"Well, we'd better go back, hadn't we?"

"Oh, not yet—of course not. We'll try it a riffle, first."

"Suppose, now—this is merely a supposition, you know—suppose you could find a ledge that would yield, say, a hundred and fifty dollars a ton—would that satisfy you?"

"Try us once!" from the whole party.

"Or suppose—merely a supposition, of course—suppose you were to find a ledge that would yield two thousand dollars a ton—would *that* satisfy you?"

"Here—what do you mean? What are you coming at? Is there some mystery behind all this?"

"Never mind. I am not saying anything. You know perfectly well there are no rich mines here—of course you do. Because you have been around and examined for yourselves. Anybody would know that, that had been around. But just for the sake of argument, suppose—in a kind of general way—suppose some person were to tell you that two-thousand-dollar ledges were simply contemptible—contemptible, understand—and that right yonder in sight of this very cabin there were piles of pure gold and pure silver—oceans of it—enough to make you all rich in twenty-four hours! Come!"

"I should say he was as crazy as a loon!" said old Ballou, but wild with excitement, nevertheless.

"Gentlemen," said I, "I don't say anything—*I* haven't been around, you know, and of course don't know anything—but all I ask of you is to cast your eye on *that*, for instance, and tell me what you think of it!" and I tossed my treasure before them.

There was an eager scrabble for it, and a closing of heads together over it under the candlelight. Then old Ballou said:

"Think of it? I think it is nothing but a lot of granite rubbish and nasty glittering mica that isn't worth ten cents an acre!"

So vanished my dream. So melted my wealth away. So toppled my airy castle to the earth and left me stricken and forlorn.

Moralizing, I observed, then, that "all that glitters is not gold."

Mr. Ballou said I could go further than that, and lay it up among my treasures of knowledge, that *nothing* that glitters is gold. So I learned then, once for all, that gold in its native state is but dull, unornamental stuff, and that only low-born metals excite the admiration of the ignorant with an ostentatious glitter. However, like the rest of the world, I still go on underrating men of gold and glorifying men of mica. Commonplace human nature cannot rise above that. . . .

from *The Conquest of the Arid West* *(1900)*

William E. Smythe

Water issues have been a constant factor in Nevada history. In 1902 Congressman Francis G. Newlands sponsored legislation creating the federal reclamation program, and shortly thereafter the Truckee-Carson Irrigation District was constructed, the first of many projects in the arid West. Newlands and his supporters drew considerable strength from the euphoric predictions about the potential of such projects turning the Nevada desert green. Some of the most influential were written by the eastern born and educated progressive journalist, William E. Smythe. His views are cogently summarized in the selections taken from his influential book, The Conquest of the Arid West, *first published in 1900.*

The Better Half of the United States

The ninety-seventh meridian divides the United States almost exactly into halves. East of that line dwell seventy-five million people. Here are overgrown cities and overcrowded industries. Here is surplus capital, as idle and burdensome as the surplus population. West of that line dwell five or six millions—less than the population of Pennsylvania, and scarcely more than that of Greater New York. And yet the vast territory to the West—so little known, so lightly esteemed, so sparsely peopled—is distinctly the better half of the United States.

The West and East are different sections, not merely in name and geographical location, but in physical endowments and fundamental elements of economic life. Nature wrote upon them, in her own indelible characters, the story of their wide contrasts and the prophecy of their varying civilizations. To the one were given the advantages of earlier development, but for the other were reserved the opportunities of a riper time. It was the destiny of the one to blossom and fruit in an epoch distinguished for the accumulation of wealth, with its vast possibilities of evil and of good. It was the destiny of the other to lie fallow until humanity should feel a nobler impulse; then to nurse, in the shadow of its everlasting mountains and the warmth of its unfailing sunshine, new dreams of liberty and equality for men.

That this is not the popular conception of the mission of the Far West may be frankly acknowledged. The region is little known to the great middle-classes in American life. It has been demonstrated by actual statistics that only three per cent of our people travel more than fifty miles from their homes in the course of a year. Those who make extended pleasure tours gravitate not unnaturally to Europe, drawn by the fascination of quaint foreign scenes and the fame of historic places. But the comparatively few whose business or fancy has taken them across the continent fail, as a rule, to grasp the true significance of the wide empire which stretches from the middle of the great plains to the shores of the Western sea.

It is a common human instinct to regard unfamiliar conditions with distrust. The first settlers in Iowa engaged in desperate rivalry for possession of the wooded lands, thinking that no soil was fit for agricultural purposes unless it furnished the pioneer an opportunity to cut down trees and pull up stumps. "Land that won't grow trees won't grow anything," was the maxim of the knowing ones. Their fathers had cleared the forests on the slopes of the Alleghenies to make way for the plough and the field, and the new generation could not conceive that land which bore rich crops of wild grasses and lay plastic and level for the husbandman to begin his labors, could have any value. A great deal of hard work was wasted before it was discovered that nature had provided new and superior conditions in the land beyond the Mississippi.

So it generally happens that the casual Western traveler, looking at the country from car-windows in the intervals between his daily paper, brings back more contempt than admiration for the economic possibilities of the country. One must live in the Far West to begin to comprehend it. Not only so, but he must come with eager eyes from an older civilization, and he must study the beginnings of industrial and social institutions throughout the region as a whole, to have any adequate appreciation of the real potentialities of that half of the United States which has been reserved for the theatre of twentieth-century developments. To all other observers the new West is a sealed book.

The West is divided from the East by a boundary-line which is not imaginary. It is a plain mark on the face of the earth, and no man made it. It is the place where the region of assured rainfall ends and the arid region begins. . . .

The superiority of the western half-continent over its eastern counterpart may not be expressed in a word. It is, rather, a matter for patient unfolding through a study of natural conditions over wide areas, and a scrutiny of the human institutions which are the inevitable product of this environment. Aridity, in the elementary sense, is purely an affair of climate. That it is also the germ of new industrial and social systems, with far-reaching possibilities in the fields of ethics and politics, will be demonstrated further on in these pages. But the first item of importance in the assets of the new West is climate. . . .

The Rising State of Nevada

Nevada, after a period of stagnation and decline, is moving along the upward path with steady strides and stands well to the front among States which are conspicuously prosperous.

No mining camps are attracting wider attention than Tonopah, Goldfield, and Bullfrog. No new agricultural district is more prominently in the eye of the home seeker than Carson Valley, watered by the first government canal to reach completion. No railroad developments now in progress promise more revolutionary results in opening rich, but hitherto idle, natural resources to human conquest, than the "Clark Road," which traverses the neglected empire of southern Nevada, the Western Pacific, which is to cross the State from east to west, and the lines which have been extended into the new and flourishing mining camps near the southwestern border. And few indeed are the towns which show a stronger pulse-beat than Reno, the commercial capital of the State.

No division of the Union has been so persistently and grossly misunderstood as the big sage-brush commonwealth which lies between Utah and California—two States of unusual human interest. The popular impression of Nevada has been largely created by those whose opinion of its scenery and resources is based on their experience of a railroad flight across its wide expanse. They glance impatiently out of the car window, inhale some alkali dust, and then denounce the region as "only fit to hold the earth together." If they happen to be literary artists, they vent their disgust in some such striking phrases as these, employed by a popular writer in a recent novel:

> "For beauty and promise, Nevada is a name among names. Nevada! Pronounce the word aloud. Does it not evoke mountains and clear air, heights of untrodden snow and valleys aromatic with the pine and musical with falling waters? Nevada! But the name is all. Abomination of desolation presides over nine-tenths of the place. The sun beats down on a roof of zinc, fierce and dull. Not a drop of water to a mile of sand. The mean ash-dump landscape stretches on from nowhere to nowhere, a spot of mange. No portion of the earth is more lacquered with paltry, unimportant ugliness."

What a difference in human souls! The man who sees a "spot of mange" in God's handiwork only reflects the spot of mange within himself, and shows how his own intelligence is "lacquered with paltry, unimportant ugliness." John C. Van Dyke looks upon the same scenes and then writes, in that classic, "The Desert:"

> "Not in vain these wastes of sand. And this time not because they develop character in desert life, but simply because they are beautiful in themselves and good to look upon whether they be life or death. In sublimity—the superlative degree of beauty—

what land can equal the desert with its wide plains, its grim mountains, and its expanding canopy of sky! You shall never see elsewhere as here the dome, the pinnacle, the minaret fretted with golden fire at sunrise and sunset; you shall never see elsewhere as here the sunset valleys swimming in a pink and lilac haze, the great mesas and plateaus fading into blue distance, the gorges and canyons banked full of purple shadow. Never again shall you see such light and air and color; never such opaline mirage, such rosy dawn, such fiery twilight. . . . Look out from the mountain's edge once more. A dusk is gathering on the desert's face, and over the eastern horizon the purple shadow of the world is reaching up to the sky. The light is fading out. Plain and mesa are blurring into unknown distances, and mountain-ranges are looming dimly into unknown heights. Warm drifts of lilac-blue are drawn like mists across the valleys; the yellow sands have shifted into a pallid gray. The glory of the wilderness has gone down with the sun. Mystery—that haunting sense of the unknown—is all that remains."

The difference between these two authors is only a difference in development. The one beholds a sealed book; the other understands. Nevada is typical of the whole desert region between the Rockies and the Western Ocean. To those who cannot comprehend its strange ensemble it is undeniably ugly, but to those who can comprehend, it is a land stamped with a beauty full of endless surprises. These latter are not necessarily cultured Van Dykes. They may be men who have never studied art or even read a book. Many a Piute Indian has looked upon the deserts and mountains of Nevada with a comprehension utterly denied to the novelist who beholds nothing in the scene except a "mean ash-dump landscape."

Even the fleeting railroad tourist might correct his superficial impression of Nevada's worthlessness by getting out of the car occasionally. Let him step off for a few moments to enjoy the cool fragrance of the little oasis at Humboldt, to walk within the shade of its trees and hear the music of its waters. The little patch of green which a hillside spring has spoken into being is a sample of what millions of desert acres will become. Farther on, the westbound traveler catches a twilight glimpse of the thriving farms of Lovelock or the green Truckee meadows. But the larger examples of irrigation lie off the beaten path. Such an instance is the Carson Valley, hidden between the sheltering shoulders of the Sierras. To appreciate the possibilities of the region, the critic should visit that valley in the perfect Nevada springtime and look upon its farms, its homes, and its villages. There he would behold a memorable picture of thrift, of beauty, and of peace, from the white blossoms in the dooryards to the white summits of the mountains, and there he might read the true prophecy of Nevada's future.

Nevada farmers are very prosperous on the average, taking one year with another, and probably much more so than the farmers in more pretentious localities. For the most part, they were poor when they came and have grown steadily better off. The climate is perfectly adapted to the production of all the cereals and hardy fruits. The wheat is perfect, with a full, rich kernel and a clean, golden straw, free from smut and rust. It has taken prizes at all the great expositions. With a variety of soil, on the different slopes of hillside, plain, and valley, there are conditions to meet almost every requirement in an agricultural way within the limitations of climate. It seems absurd to explain that Nevada does not produce oranges, yet the question is sometimes asked by those who only know that Nevada is the next-door neighbor of California. Speaking broadly, Nevada is an elevated plateau in the Great Basin enclosed by the Wasatch Range on the east and the Sierra on the west, having an average altitude of about four thousand feet. Its climate is that of the north temperate zone. The winter is cold, the summer hot, the springtime marked by showers and high wind, the autumn long and golden. As in other parts of the arid region, the dry air moder-

ates cold and heat, giving man and vegetation the benefits arising from the vigorous qualities of these extremes without the unpleasant effects which are felt in humid districts.

The national irrigation projects in Nevada are described in a later chapter, but it is important to note here the influence which this development must inevitably exert upon the
whole social, political, and commercial life of the State. There will be a steady influx of
population for many years to come. Farms will be smaller and more intensively cultivated.
There will be a corresponding expansion in all lines of business. Social life in the country
will lose its frontier characteristics, and political power will gravitate largely into the hands
of the hosts of newcomers, drawn from many different parts of the United States. Owing
their opportunities to the first great national experiment in the public ownership of utilities
essential to industrial development, it would be strange indeed if this new population—the
dominant element of the future—does not favor very advanced ideas in politics. . . .

Standing on the height above the roaring Truckee at Reno, in the midst of fragrant alfalfa fields and well fruited orchards, but little imagination is required to behold the Nevada of the future which is now rapidly rising on the Nevada of the past. A big, splendid,
American State, blest with the climate in which English-speaking man has won nearly all
his triumphs, except that its skies are cleared by aridity and its sunshine brightened by altitude, a land full of prosperous little farms, tilled by their owners, mountains pouring out
their annual tribute of gold and silver, towns large enough to offer the refinements of modern life yet small enough to escape the awful contrasts between superfluous wealth and
hopeless poverty, and a people so economically freed and politically untrammeled that
they may make their institutions what they will,—this is the Nevada of the future. . . .

Truckee-Carson Project, Nevada

What is known as "the Truckee-Carson project" will ultimately irrigate 375,000 acres at a
cost of about $9,000,000. Nine years will be required to bring it to completion. The portion
of the works put into operation on June 17th, 1905, will distribute water to about 50,000
acres and represents a cost of about $1,750,000.

The main canal now in operation diverts the water from the channel of the Truckee at a
point twenty-four miles east of Reno and conveys it through the divide to the Carson River,
a distance of thirty-one miles. This canal has a capacity for the first six miles of its course of
1400 cubic feet per second, or 70,000 miner's inches under a four-inch pressure, and, for the
remainder of its course, of 1200 cubic feet per second. There are three tunnels, all lined with
concrete, as are two miles of the canal outside of the tunnels. The main canal discharges its
water into a natural reservoir on the Carson and flows thence four and one-half miles to the
diversion dam at the head of the distributing system, where it is led out upon the land in
two wide-reaching canals, one on each side of the river. The canal on the north side has a
capacity of 450 cubic feet per second. With their main branches, these waterways will ultimately have a total length of over 90 miles, while the laterals and drain-ditches to be constructed in Carson Sink Valley alone will aggregate fully 1200 miles.

The dam in the Carson at the head of the distributing system is something to bring a
smile of satisfaction to the faces of those who have known the crude brush dams of the
pioneers and the endless difficulties which arose from them. This government dam is a
solid concrete structure, built for a thousand years. It furnishes an absolute guaranty of a
permanent water supply to the settlers. This, indeed, is the character of all the work the
Government has done.

The land to be irrigated is located in a number of valleys along the Truckee and Carson Rivers, extending on each side from the Central Pacific Railroad, the greatest distance from the road being twenty-five miles. The soil is adapted to alfalfa and other forage crops, potatoes, onions, beets, and other vegetables, apples, pears, berries, and similar hardy fruit.

Nearly all the land now irrigated was public property until recently filed upon, after the works were undertaken. Some of it is still open, but this condition will not continue long. No price is charged for the land, except filing fees, which are nominal. But the settler must repay the cost of irrigation in ten annual installments, without interest. This amounts to $26 an acre, of which about $10 an acre has been incurred by the provision of drainage facilities, made imperatively necessary as a means of removing the heavy alkali deposits. The settler is fortunate to be able to make his home where conditions have been scientifically ascertained in advance and where the best engineering skill, together with abundant capital, have been available to make the most thorough preparation for his success. . . .

"Prelude" from
City of Trembling Leaves
(1945)

Walter Van Tilburg Clark

Born in the East but raised in Reno where his father was the long-time president of the University of Nevada, Walter Van Tilburg Clark established himself in the first echelon of American writers during the middle of the twentieth century. His novels, The Ox-Bow Incident *(1940) and the* Track of the Cat *(1949), received critical acclaim and both were adapted for feature motion pictures. Clark's* City of Trembling Leaves *(1945) provides a poignant treatment of the transition from childhood to adulthood and was based in the small city in which he grew up. His Prelude to this novel provides a glimpse at a side of Nevada life that has all but disappeared under the avalanche of growth and the forces of modernity.*

Prelude

This is the story of the lives and loves of Timothy Hazard, and so, indirectly, a token biography of Reno, Nevada, as well. Now, whatever else Reno may be, and it is many things, it is the city of trembling leaves. The most important meaning of leaves is the same everywhere in Reno, of course, and everywhere else, for that matter, which is what Tim implies when he calls moribund any city containing a region in which you can look all around and not see a tree. Such a city is drawing out of its alliance with the eternal, with the Jurassic Swamps and the Green Mansions, and in time it will also choke out the trees in the magic wilderness of the spirit. In Reno, however, this universal importance of trees is intensified, for Reno is in the Great Basin of America, between the Rockies and the Sierras, where the vigor of the sun and the height of the mountains, to say nothing of the denuding activities of mining booms, have created a latter-day race of tree worshippers. Furthermore, to such tree worshippers, and Tim Hazard is high in the cult, the trees of Reno have regional meanings within their one meaning, like the themes and transitions of a one-movement symphony. It would be impossible to understand Tim Hazard without hearing these motifs played separately before you hear them in the whole.

The trees of the Wingfield Park-Court Street region dispense an air of antique melancholy. You become sad and old as you walk under these trees, even on a bright, winter day when all the leaves are gone and the branches make only narrow shadows across homes covered with sunlight.

The park is not large, yet it feels like the edge of a wilderness of infinite extent, so that if you lie on the grass there on Sunday, or sit on one of the green benches (this is in the summer now), you don't even have to close your eyes to believe in a great depth of forest and shadow of time. In part this is due to the illusion that the treetops of Reno are continuous, one elevated pampas of stirring leaves, unconcerned with houses and streets below, so that the park, actually a ledge between the Truckee River and the bluff of Court Street, does not seem set apart. Even more it is due to the spacious shadow and the quiet under the trees. No rush of wind and leaves, no slow snowing of cottonwood-down, or cries of playing children, or running on the tennis courts can really disturb this quiet. It is an everlasting late-afternoon somnolence, the mood of a Watteau painting, if you can imagine the beribboned courtiers much smaller under their trees, like Corot's wood nymphs, and completely dreamy, not even toying with flutes, mandolins, fruit or amorous preliminaries. This applies only to the older part of the park, of course. The newer part, on the island breasting the Truckee, is out in the sun, and its trees are younger and more susceptible to vagrant airs. It is like a light motif dropped into the melancholy central movement in anticipation of the theme of the outskirts.

The mood of the Court Street trees is heavy with the homes, some of which can be seen from below, staring northward from the bluff out of tired windows. Among their lawns, shaded by their trees and their pasts, these houses do not wholly despair, but they have reason to. Their doors seem closed, their windows empty and still, and they appear to meditate upon longer, more intricate and more pathetic pasts than any of them could possibly have accumulated. The vitality of these houses, compounded of memory and discontent, is inconsiderable compared with their resignation. Even though it would not be statistically accurate, you must think of all the houses in Court Street in terms of high-ceilinged rooms with the shades drawn in late afternoon in summer, or with the shades up but the windows closed in a windy, moonlit night in winter. And you must be alone in the room and in the house. It makes no difference any more who lives in these houses, or what they do; they cannot change this nature, which has been accepted and expressed by the trees of Court Street.

Beyond Court Street to the south, this mood goes through a gradual and almost constant brightening. The Court Street theme still dominates the region of Flint, Hill, Liberty, Granite and California, all that height and slope between Belmont Road and Virginia Street, the region of big rooming houses and apartments, which owes allegiance to the Washoe County Court House, and may be called the Court House Quarter. Even the private homes of this region are sunk under the Court Street theme, and its big and beautiful trees give the impression that they should be motionless, even in a plateau gale, and that only their topmost leaves should accept sunlight, and tremble. Tim's best friend, Lawrence Black, whose life will at times seem almost synonymous with Tim's, lived in this quarter when he was a boy, and Tim says that his home echoed the theme, and was gently and completely haunted from attic to basement. Its liveliest time was the bearable melancholy of six o'clock in the afternoon in June. Tim's great single love, Rachel Wells, also lived in this quarter, in a big house with porte-cochere and an air of dark yesterdays, until she had finished high school.

From here out, to the south and west, spreads a high region of increasingly new homes, bungalows, ornamented brick structures of greater size, a number of which it would be difficult to describe fairly, and white, Spanish houses. This region seems to become steadily more open, windy and sunlit as you move out, and at some point you will realize that the Court Street theme has become inaudible, and that you have truly entered what may be called the Mt. Rose Quarter. Here there are many new trees, no taller than a man, always trembling so they nearly dance, and most of the grown trees are marching files of poplars, in love with wind and heavens. Here, no matter how many houses rear up, stark in the sunlight, you remain more aware of the sweeping domes of earth which hold them down, and no matter how long you stay in one of the houses, you will still be more aware of Mt. Rose aloft upon the west, than of anything in the house: furniture, silver, books, or even people. Even at night, when the summit of the mountain is only a starlit glimmer, detached from earth, it is the strong pole of all waking minds in that quarter.

I do not mean to celebrate newness as such, any more than I would celebrate oldness as such. Temporal age is unimportant. There is a strong likeness between many old houses, brownstone, brick and Victorian frame, and the brand-new gas works, factories and warehouses which quickly create moribund districts in a city, districts from which life, if it has any choice, shies away. It is rather that this Mt. Rose region is more open to the eternal and reproductive old. It may be significant, for instance, though doubtless it galls a few property owners, whose interest in earth is in marking it into salable squares, that part way out Plumas Street, which is the main thoroughfare of the Mt. Rose quarter, there is still a farm, with a brook in its gully, cows on its steep slopes, and a sign on a tree saying EGGS FOR SALE. It may also be significant that Tim Hazard and his gentle, golden-brown wife Mary, live in one of the small bungalows about halfway out Plumas, not far beyond the Billinghurst School, and on the east side of the street, so that Tim can sit on the front steps and look at Mt. Rose while he waters the lawn, and Mary can see it through the kitchen window while she works at the sink. It may even be significant, for that matter, that the Hazards live in a bungalow. Such houses, the easiest in the world to forget, are infinitely mutable under the impact of the thoughts, dreams, desires and acts of the people living in them, while in houses like those on Court Street there is great danger that the shaping will be reversed. Houses are incipiently evil which have been intended to master time and dominate nature. That is a moribund intention. It feels death coming on all the time, and, having no faith in reproduction or multiplicity, tries to build a fort to hold it off.

On the north side of the Truckee River, the Court Street theme continues, but in a higher and sharper key, interrupted by short, ominous passages from the middle of the city. Also it moves toward the north edge more rapidly and with a quickening tempo, for in this district of the McKinley Park and Mary S. Doten schools, the dominant houses are, from the first, the dying miniature Victorian and the bungalows, and they don't influence the trees.

When you reach the little trees of the north edge, where Virginia Street becomes the Purdy Road, or the region of upper Ralston Street west of the hilltop cemeteries, there is a new theme, higher, clearer and sharper than that of the south edge. Here the city is thinner, and not expanding so rapidly, for it is already on the mountains. From windows on the heights, University Terrace, College Drive, Fourteenth and Fifteenth Streets, you look down across the whole billowing sea of the treetops of Reno, and feel more removed from the downtown section than in any other place in the city, because you are off any main streets, away from the sound of them even, and because you can see the tops of downtown places, the Medico-Dental Building, the roof sign of the Riverside Hotel, the gray breasts of the Catholic Church, like strange and tiny islands in that sea, and realize how far you are from them.

There is another difference, too, which indirectly affects the meaning of the trees. The University of Nevada is on the climbing north edge, and it is an even better place than any of the parks for glens and stretches of lawn, and clumps and avenues of trees. It has a tone of active, enduring quiet, and is big enough to impart much of this tone to all the north, except the eastern corner, which is drawn into the influence of the race track. For Tim Hazard, after his boyhood, the university quarter was foreign country, the city of the hills seen from the plains. He went up there only once in a while, to hear some music, or see a play, or watch a game in the gymnasium or on Mackay Field. Yet he says that he always felt that in going north, toward the university, he should walk, but in going south, until he had passed the last service station on the South Virginia Road, he should drive, and drive like hell.

A further and, perhaps, in the course of time, even more important, difference between the high north edge, and the low south edge, is that Mt. Rose is the sole, white, exalted patron angel and foundation of wind and storm to south Reno, while in north Reno, her reign is strongly contested by black Peavine Mountain, less austere, wilder, and the home of two winds. Mt. Rose is a detached goal of the spirit, requiring a lofty and difficult worship. Peavine is the great, humped child of desert. He is barren, and often lowering, but he reaches out and brings unto him, while Rose stands aloof. He is part of the great plateau which is the land of the city, while Rose is part of the western barrier. Rose begets reverence, but Peavine begets love. There is a liveliness in his quarter which gets into everything. . . .

The north-east quarter of Reno, with the ranching valley on the east of it and the yellow hills with a few old mines on the north, is drawn out of the influence of the university and Peavine into the vortex of the race track. Even in Tim's boyhood the race track was alive only two or three weeks out of a year, yet it seems a fast-moving place. The trembling of the leaves in its sphere rises easily into a roaring through tall Lombardies set in rows in dust and open sunlight. This quality of thin, hasty brightness persists clear down through the quarter, where the trees close in and the small, white houses fill the blocks, in the lumber yard beyond, and even down to the Western Pacific Depot and the grimy edge of Fourth Street. It is a theme almost strident, and saved from being as intolerable as persistent whistles only by the yellow hills, like cats asleep in the north, and by the greater and darker

Virginia Range in the east, through which the Truckee cuts its red and shadowy gorge. Sunset on those hills is also a very important subduer. . . .

The south-east quarter of Reno combines the qualities of the north-east and south-west, yet has a quite different, quieter and more uniform tone, because it is dedicated to the valley, into which it is slowly spreading, and is not much influenced by any mountain. Daybreak and sunset are the test times of any region's allegiance, and at daybreak and sunset the south-east quarter thinks toward the valley, where the light spreads widely, and is more aware of that level spaciousness than of the mountains beyond it. None of the themes of Reno is isolated, however. They merge one into another, and so one corner of this quarter, the Mill Street toward Virginia Street corner, echoes the Court Street theme and the rumbling and cries of the center of the city.

Reno began with Lake's Crossing on the Truckee, and in its beginnings was divided by the Truckee, but as it grew the activity of men quartered it by the intersection of Virginia Street, running more or less north and south, and Fourth Street, running more or less east and west. Virginia Street and Fourth Street are what is commonly called the main arteries, or the purveyors of the life-blood of the city. They are the streets which continue on out and tie Reno into the world, as the others fade away or blend into each other. The only important difference between them and the purveyors of the life-blood of any city arises from the fact that Reno has sheltered itself in the north-west corner of its valley, so that it has stretched along Virginia Street only to the south, where it becomes the highway to Carson, and along Fourth Street only to the east, where Reno and Sparks have become practically one city. It is more important, however, to the Reno of Tim Hazard, that on the west, Fourth Street plunges quickly into the foothills of the Sierras, and that North Virginia Street promptly becomes the Purdy Road, which goes away lonesomely across passes and great desert valleys into a land of timber, fine cattle, deep upland meadows and secret lakes. It is notable, for instance, that on the Purdy Road hawks, and even eagles, may be seen perching for long periods on fence posts and telephone poles.

Mary Turner lived in a frame bungalow on North Virginia Street, opposite the university, while she and Tim were going to the Orvis Ring School. The Orvis Ring is the school for the north-east quarter. The Western Pacific tracks run right behind it, but the Western Pacific there is a quiet, single line, and doesn't disturb the school, or have much effect on the quarter, except as a dividing line between the university region and the racetrack region.

This is not the case with the big Southern Pacific lines, but since they run through the downtown section, and only a block south of Fourth Street, they don't create a separate zone. Aside from the fact that they make a railroad street of Commercial Row, their effect is one with that of Fourth Street. Yet they have a subtle influence in Reno, whether it is heeded or not, aside, that is, from the obvious results of carrying thousands of people and cattle, and thousands of tons of freight, into and out of and through Reno. The gigantic freight engines of the Southern Pacific, often two to a train when headed into the mountains, gently shake all the windows in the city in their passage. At night their tremendous mushrooms of smoke, lighted from beneath by the center of the city, may be seen from the hills of the north edge, swelling above the trees. Their wild whistles cry in the night, and echo mournfully all round the mountain walls of the valley. Thus Reno is reminded constantly that it is only one small stop on the road of the human world, that it trembles with the comings and goings of that world, and yet that the greatest cry of that world is only a brief echo against mountains.

Mary told me once that the whistles of the big steam engines were so sad that when they woke her at night, in the bungalow on North Virginia, and she heard their echoes still slowly circling the valley and dying, she would sometimes even cry a little, and would invariably begin on long thoughts of loneliness and mortality. This confession is significant, because Mary is a contented person, wise in the small, permanent ways, and her childhood home was much more peaceful than Tim's. Her father was a short, quiet man, who worked on the university grounds and did a little business in taxidermy in a shed behind the house. Her mother was a plump, affectionate woman, and a very good cook, whose chief interest, aside from her family, was in several varieties of roses, which she made to grow over the house, over the green-lattice fence between the house and the shed, and in clumps about the lawn and the steps. It is enough to indicate the peace of Mary's home that her father took up taxidermy for the secret reason that he hated to think of so many lovely creatures leaving no tangible memories, that her mother always wrote for a dozen seed catalogues when the first thaw came in February, and that the three of them often sat together silently on the front porch in the summer evenings and watched the last light slowly ascend the trees on the university campus.

There is also, of course, the treeless center of the city, which we have worked all around, though not without hearing it several times, in sudden, shrill bursts from the brass or deep mutterings in the rhythm section. This, however, is the region about which the world already knows or imagines more, in a Sunday-supplement way, than is true, and it will do, for the present, to suggest that it is not unlike any moribund city, or the moribund region of any city. It is the ersatz jungle, where the human animals, uneasy in the light, dart from cave to cave under steel and neon branches, where the voice of the croupier halloos in the secret glades, and high and far, like light among the top leaves, gleam the names of lawyers and hairdressers on upstairs windows. In short, this is the region which may be truly entered by passing under the arch which says, RENO, THE BIGGEST LITTLE CITY IN THE WORLD.

Yet there is one important difference between even this region and the truly moribund cities of the world, the difference which makes Reno a city of adolescence, a city of dissonant themes, sawing against each other with a kind of piercing beauty like that of a fourteen-year-old girl or a seventeen-year-old boy, the beauty of everything promised and nothing resolved. Even from the very center of Reno, from the intersection of Virginia and Second Streets, and even at night, when restless club lights mask the stars, one can look in any direction and see the infinite shoals of the leaves hovering about the first lone crossing light.

"What Has Wide-Open Gambling Done to Nevada?"
(1952)

Robert Laxalt

Robert Laxalt was born in 1923 to Basque immigrant parents. His father, Dominique, spent much of his time in the Sierra mountains tending to his sheep, while his mother Theresa raised their six children while operating a Basque hotel in Carson City. After graduating from the University of Nevada in 1947, Laxalt covered Nevada for the Associated Press. He also published more than 200 articles in prominent national magazines, including a series on Nevada landscapes in National Geographic. *He received national acclaim for* Sweet Promised Land *(1957), a nonfiction book that described the emotional visit of his aging father to his native Basque country. Several novels followed that described aspects of the Nevada and Basque experience including* A Man in the Wheatfield *(1964),* A Cup of Tea in Pamploma *(1985),* The Basque Hotel *(1989), and* The Governor's Mansion *(1994). Laxalt's first national publication dealt with the many issues raised by Nevada's growing gambling industry and appeared in 1952 in* The Saturday Evening Post.

In the year 1931, an Eastern newspaper editor said, "If you can't do it at home, go to Nevada." The reason for the quip was that Nevada had just shocked the moral boot tops off the nation by legalizing gambling. The action was not born of madness. There was an argument for it. But in the furor of outraged criticism that followed, that timid voice of argument was hopelessly lost. It was only when the verbal smoke had finally cleared that the question arose, "How did this thing come to be?"

The answer did not lie in an economic maze, but simply in the fact that Nevada liked to pride herself on liberal tolerance. "Have done with hypocrisy!" her lawmakers stated. "Get gambling out of the back rooms and into the daylight."

Which is exactly what happened. The green felted tables crept into the neighborhood bars and lounges. Slot machines made a brassy appearance in grocery stores. And casinos suddenly flared into being with dazzling displays of roulette wheels, craps and 21 tables.

It is hardly likely that the crusading liberals of the Nevada of 1931 were clairvoyant. They could not have foreseen the repercussions of their action—repercussions that were to sound the biggest boom the state had known since the mining heyday of the Comstock lode.

In the years that followed, the mechanized tourist was to come of age. It was only natural that he should turn his head toward the West, its little-known scenic grandeur, its shockingly vast expanse, and of course, its "rip-roaring wide-open Nevada." By this time the moral taboo was off and the nation had swallowed a bitter pill.

Now, twenty-one years later, gambling has again shifted to the limelight. Crime-investigation committees, so-called syndicated gangsterism and bookies are all common fare in the language of today. And again, Nevada has come under the sharp scrutiny of a nationwide society of crime watchers. It rests in an uncertain vacuum. Twenty-one years of legalized gambling. What has it accomplished for Nevada? Has it been a success or a failure?

Economically speaking, legalized gambling has been a success. Take a look at the facts. Two decades ago, this sprawling desert state—with only 12 percent of her 110,000 square miles privately owned—had no economic future. Its population stood at a mere 91,000, actually less than one person per square mile. Its once fabulous mining industry had reached a new low. There were minimum prospects in livestock and agriculture. Industry was undreamed of. Touristry was not yet fully born, but even if it had been, the scenic advantages of a barren sagebrush state were laughable.

But in one stroke, legalization of gambling was to make this final category—touristry—easily the foremost in Nevada's economy. In the year 1951, for example, an estimated 3,000,000 tourists through Reno stayed an average of three days apiece and spent more than $32,000,000. Las Vegas, in Southern Nevada, boasting year-round sunshine and semi-tropical climate, scaled higher. Nearly 2,500,000 tourists stayed an average of four days apiece and spent $43,000,000.

Behold the Tourist "Just Passing Through"

The cycle is always the same. Mr. Average Tourist points the nose of his car west. No matter if he plans a trip to the Southwest, to California or the Pacific Northwest, something else comes first—most often Reno or Las Vegas. Here lie glittering gambling halls, silver dollars stacked high, croupiers and shills, back-room gambling flaunted openly in lavish casinos.

Perhaps he had planned only to drive through and take a quick look. But an outing to the gambling clubs takes time. There are too many wheels and tables to be seen. There are timid experimental bets of a dollar or fifty cents across the green felt or a few nickels in the slot machines, just to say that "I gave the gambling a whirl."

Quite without his being aware of it, lunchtime has rolled around. And after lunch, a trip to another club or a glimpse of the town of legend, "as long as I'm here." There's the inevitable purchase of a souvenir, then dinner, and "as long as I'm here this late, I might as well stay tonight."

This means a hotel or motel, lubrication for the car, a movie or a night out around the town. If he's stopped in Reno, the next morning usually brings a trip to nearby Virginia City or a visit to the tiniest capital in the nation—Carson City. And so on, until the number of merchants benefiting from the brief stop has mounted to an unbelievable figure.

Now, if there were no gambling, the average tourist would do everything in his power to bypass the sagebrush state of Nevada and her hundreds of miles of scorching waste. If by chance he managed to pass through Reno or Las Vegas en route to California, he would merely slow down his car and gaze curiously around.

"Not much different from any other town," he would mutter. "Same buildings, same stores, same movies."

He would see a woman on the street and wonder idly if she was a divorcee. They certainly aren't on display, so there would be no way of knowing. His car would reach the city limits and he would be off to California. From the viewpoint of the merchant, there's a frighteningly wide gap between the two instances.

Then there are the celebrations. Nevada celebrations are carnival affairs, planned in almost every case around a rodeo and Wild West theme. Held during the summer, they would attract not only tourists but a parade of visitors from neighboring states of California, Utah, Idaho, Oregon and Arizona.

Accommodations are almost impossible to find at the height of one of these celebrations. Hotels, motels and rooming houses are filled to capacity, and chambers of commerce even appeal to private residents for rooms.

For the annual Reno Rodeo alone—a four-day affair over the Fourth of July—an estimated 20,000 visitors jam the town like a beehive, wildly spending $500,000 in their furious stay. Las Vegas' Helldorado celebration runs a close second, with 18,000 visitors pouring out slightly less than $500,000 over a three-day period. . . .

The same applies to conventions. During the past few years, more and more national associations and societies have been making it a practice to hold annual conventions in Nevada—again for the added promise of a good time. For example, Reno boasted nearly sixty conventions and some 15,000 delegates last year. Their spending power again ranged near the $500,000 mark. Las Vegas drew 6,000 visitors to twenty-two conventions. Their money output—$160,000.

Naturally, these three categories—touristry, celebrations and conventions—have prompted the construction of multimillion-dollar hotels, elaborate resorts, night clubs, and more casinos. In Reno and Las Vegas combined there are nearly a dozen $1,000,000 hotels. And both are small towns. Their population ranges only to the 30,000 figure.

Looking at Nevada from its own viewpoint, however, the population increase has been unnatural since legalization of gambling. Today it stands nearly double what it was in 1931, or around 165,000 residents. The other by-products of the experiment range all the way from high real-estate values to a surprising $25,000,000 yearly payroll in hotels, gambling casinos and night clubs.

From the time gambling was legalized in Nevada, it was a full fourteen years before the state government took a direct tax look at the industry. From 1931 until 1945, all the state derived from its gambling was a scant 25 percent share of token license fees levied by the counties. The total state share was about $30,000 a year.

But in the few years preceding 1945, Nevada lawmakers found themselves faced with big problems. The population was increasing by leaps and bounds. More school buildings were urgently needed. The highway program needed expansion, and state institutions were in sad need of repair.

During this time, more and more lawmakers had been casting glances at the gambling industry and its gilt-edged betting volume—a volume that was approaching the $1,000,000,000-a-year level. So by 1945 one lawmaking faction openly argued that gamblers should be taxed for the privilege of operating under state protection.

Opponents of the move rallied around two flags of counterargument: one, that Nevada should hold fast to her "hands-off-tainted-money" tradition, speaking taxwise; and two, that the state would be foolhardy to allow her tax structure to become entangled with such an uncertain industry, an industry that could fluctuate sharply. Their case was supported by the depression year of 1933, when gambling volume had been cut in half.

After weeks of torrid debate, a compromise solution was reached. An experimental tax of 1 percent of all gross gambling receipts would be levied. And in a somewhat feeble and devious gesture against the tainted-money argument, this gambling-tax income would be deposited in the general fund, there to be channeled into various state agencies.

The financial success of the tax surpassed all expectations. In the first biennium, the state's take was over $500,000.

With the moral argument settled, the 1947 legislature doubled the tax to 2 percent and imposed a sliding-scale table fee. Since that time, Nevada has been collecting $1,000,000 a year from her gambling industry.

In legislative discussion it is still spoken of as "extra money." But this is far from the truth. For today nearly 20 percent of Nevada's tax income is from gambling. Only general-property taxes exceed this category as a source of income.

Counties and cities are in no better condition. With the imposition of license fees, special table levies, slot-machine taxes, both political subdivisions count on gambling for as high as 16 percent of their tax revenue.

The end result: Tax structures of three levels of government are utterly dependent upon gambling.

Contrary to general belief, Nevada has never contended that legalized gambling could work honestly and effectively in any other state. Its gambling experts point out that from every standpoint Nevada is the only ideal state for such an experiment. Her entire population would not fill one borough of a metropolitan center. And though the state is immense in area—the sixth largest in the nation—her gambling houses are relatively few. In 1951 there were only 200 actual establishments in the entire state.

Regular checks are run on these establishments by trained agents of the Nevada Tax Commission. The penalty for a dealer caught cheating is permanent banishment from the ranks of legalized gamblers; and for the gambling operator, even if he can prove no connection with the incident, at least a year's denial of a license.

Agents devote little time to the larger casinos. Common-sense reasoning shows that these big-volume establishments already have overwhelming odds in their favor. They would hardly consider taking the risk of losing a $1,000,000 business either temporarily or permanently for the sake of a few thousand dollars to be earned over a cheating table.

But the small-town saloons, the quiet cocktail lounges and the neighborhood bars are a constant headache to the gambling agent. Here he finds small-scale operators who deal their own games, operators for whom a chance to make a quick $100 by cheating is too much of a temptation.

This group of investigators came into being when the legislature delegated licensing power in 1945 to the Nevada Tax Commission, headed by a quiet, efficient public servant—Robbins Cahill. Handpicking his men on the basis of strictest character requirements, Cahill set up the first organization of its type in the history of gambling. And as it must be, his division of investigation is strictly nonpolitical. In its six-year history not the faintest rumor of corruption has stained its reputation.

The same could not hold true if gambling were legalized in a heavily populated area. With major city police forces under constant attack with charges of graft, it is easy to imagine how mass gambling and its thousand promises of quick and crooked wealth could spread corruption through the ranks of law-enforcement agencies.

When asked what effect the proximity of gambling has upon the public, too many persons dismiss the query with: "People will gamble, no matter what."

The answer is a shortsighted one. True, the inveterate gambler will gamble. In locales where gambling is not legal, he is the man who knows where every floating crap game can be found. The argument does not apply to the man of normal appetite. If there is no gambling about, he simply does not gamble.

Yet take this man of normal appetite and place him in a cocktail lounge in Nevada. All that is required for him to gamble is to walk a few steps to a table. If the table had not been there, he would not have gambled. But the simple fact of its proximity has forced the issue.

Sometimes he wins. Twenty times more often, he loses. And in the case of the average wage earner or the Saturday-night-pay-check laborer, this type of gambling hurts. In an age of slim take-home pay checks the loss of a few dollars results in a desperate attempt to recoup. Too often, he does not quit until all his money is gone, then spends weeks of penny pinching to make up the loss. Though such instances are in the minority, they nevertheless do exist. And their existence poses a moral black mark against the state.

Still, any survey in Nevada will reveal a startling fact. An overwhelming majority of residents never see the inside of a major casino or bet a single dollar during the course of several months. They see gambling every day of their lives. It holds no fascination for them. And in this sense, legalization of gambling has produced a peculiar and unexpected result.

Nevada's gamblers are a strange potpourri, ranging from the highly respectable to the extremely questionable, from the conservatively dressed to the cold-eyed, cigar-smoking prototype of the movie gangster. But until recent years this wide contrast was not existent. Practically all of Nevada's major operators fitted into the first category.

Perhaps the most striking example is Raymond I. Smith, operator of Harolds Club in Reno, second only to the casino at Monte Carlo in international-gambling reputation. Smith is a reserved, dignified man in his early sixties. He is a respected man in his community. His donations literally support a dozen churches and organizations, and he provides a yearly fund for academic scholarships to the University of Nevada, for students of promise who might otherwise never go on to higher schools. But, unfortunately, gamblers of his stripe are in the definite minority in Nevada today.

With local and national pressure flushing many illegal gamblers out of their home bailiwicks, the pendulum has swung to the other extreme. For the first time, the definite accents of New York, Chicago, Detroit and Texas can be heard on the operating end of Nevada tables. The squeeze is on, and the outside element is finding sanctuary behind the barriers of Nevada's legalized gambling.

And when this element began filtering into the state, Nevada found herself faced with a problem for which she was quite unprepared. In 1947, many Nevadans had never heard of one Benjamin (Bugsy) Siegel, and those who had, for the most part, associated him with one thing only—the $1,000,000 (Flamingo) hotel he operated in flourishing Las Vegas.

Then one night Siegel was shot to death by a gangland assassin in nearby Beverly Hills, California. And in the staggering publicity that followed, many Nevadans learned for the first time that this suave playboy was a known racketeer of international repute. It was a shock, but only the first of several to come.

The next one came from the other end of the state in the next year, when a man named Harry Sherwood was fatally shot in his plush—Tahoe Village—resort casino at Lake Tahoe. Police arrested another stranger to most Nevadans—Louis Strauss.

The first local accounts of the shooting revealed the complete ignorance of even newspaper editors about the characters who were operating the big-money casinos. The shooting was carried as a shooting, pure and simple, with no ramifications involved.

It was not until a full day later that the true identity of the principals become known. Sherwood was found to be the one-time partner of gambling-boat operator Tony Stralla, and Strauss was none other than the notorious "Russian Louie" of Eastern racket fame.

Only one year later, in 1949, a hidden assailant's shotgun blast cut down still another Nevada gambling figure, Lincoln Fitzgerald, co-owner of a Reno casino—the Nevada Club. The murder attempt failed and Fitzgerald lived, but again the name of Nevada was smeared across the nation's headlines. But by this time state editors and wire-service correspondents had prepared themselves with active files on the new names in the gambling fraternity.

The shooting was immediately laid to Michigan roots, where Fitzgerald had only recently been indicted and fined for illegal gambling.

In 1951 came the fourth incident of violence, when a gunman made an attempt on the life of Las Vegas gambler L. B. (Benny) Binion, under indictment in Texas on charges of operating a $1,000,000 numbers racket. The attempt was made shortly after the dynamite explosion that took the life of Binion's one-time arch-foe in Texas, Herbert (The Cat) Noble, for which Binion was questioned by Texas Rangers.

Throughout this reign of blood, however, the Nevada Tax Commission had not been altogether idle. Though slow in starting, it nevertheless made steady progress in controlling a situation that bordered on the uncontrollable.

First, it clarified its authority to investigate the backgrounds of all gambling applicants, to deny licenses where they were deemed to be against the public welfare. Second, it moved into the Las Vegas horse-race-wire dispute, where local distributors of the nationwide result service were either refusing more bookie customers or charging exorbitant rates. The commission removed the monopoly power from these distributors, thereby remedying an evil that threatened at any moment to flare into open violence.

Next, the commission barred horse-race bookies from accepting out-of-state bets, thus cutting off another connection between Nevada and the outside. And finally it ordered all its licensees to dispose of their out-of-state gambling interests—another move calculated to confine Nevada gambling within its own borders.

Despite this progress, the Nevada Tax Commission is under fire today for dragging its feet in cleaning up the state's gambling household. Strangely enough, the furor is stemming from Las Vegas, the very locale where gambling troubles first took root. City and county officials in the Southern Nevada area are complaining of the constant traffic of the biggest names in the racket world. They protest that underworld policy meetings have been held in various Las Vegas resort casinos. They have accused the actual membership of the commission—seven representative businessmen and officials—of bowing under pressure and public-relations efforts, to grant licenses to questionable characters. . . .

In answer to these charges and demands, the tax commission has countered that each city has the power to deny gambling licenses, regardless of the state commission's ruling. But in the maze of charges and countercharges, one healthy gleam is apparent. Nevada is aware of the gangster menace facing her gambling industry. In that awareness lies the promise of decent unrest.

Though legalized gambling has been somewhat of a moral failure, it has spelled economic prosperity for Nevada. But economic success or moral failure, Nevada has paid the inevitable price for her experiment—hopeless entanglement with gambling and all its embellishments. The state cannot discard the industry. Such a move would mean economic ruin.

Today Nevada is adapting herself to this realization. And with the realization has come the knowledge that she must insure the continued existence of gambling in Nevada. The key to this existence lies where it obviously has always lain—in the gamblers themselves. If Nevada can clean her household and keep it clean, then the future is fairly certain.

If not, economic disaster both for the state and for her gambling experiment may be very near.

"Musings of a Native Son"
(1989)

William A. Douglass

William A. Douglass has deep roots in Nevada. His professional career as a social anthropologist has included the publication of many highly acclaimed scholarly works, particularly those dealing with the Basques. He has served as the Coordinator of the unique Basque Studies program at the University of Nevada for more than two decades. Douglass also has pursued with equal energy and success a dual career as a leader of the northern Nevada gaming community, serving as part-owner of the Comstock and Riverboat hotel casinos, as well as president of the Riverboat. His introspective autobiographical essay describes growing up in the relatively small city of Reno after the Second World War, an experience that provides him a unique perspective from which to examine some of the major themes of the Nevada experience.

Times Past

My grandfather died in 1929, ten years before I was born. According to the headlined obituaries published on April 22 in the *Tonopah Daily Bonanza* and on April 23 in the *Tonopah Daily Times*, William James Douglass was one of the key founders of the town. He was born in Virginia City in 1867. His father was a mill operator from Vermont and his mother a pioneer in the mining camp of Aurora. Billy Douglass, as he was known, became an assayer in Candelaria in 1890s. With the collapse of silver prices in 1893, he and some associates went prospecting for gold. They founded Douglass Camp in Esmeralda County, which enjoyed some initial successes. In 1900, when news of the Tonopah strike reached him, Billy immediately set out across the desert, becoming the thirteenth man to enter the fledgling camp. He secured a lease from Jim Butler, and throughout the leasing period of Tonopah's history (or until late 1901 when the Butler groups sold out to eastern interests), Billy Douglass ran the local assay office. He then became a principal owner and general manager of the Midway, West End, and Tonopah Montana mines. In partnership with H. C. Brougher, he founded the Tonopah Banking Corporation and served as its vice-president. He grubstaked Harry Stimler and William Marsh, discoverers of Goldfield, and was their partner in that district's Kendall, Sandstorm, May Queen, Nevada Boy, and Gold Banner mines. He was subsequently instrumental in development of the Tonopah Divide district and had interests in several Nevada and California mining camps. With Billy's passing the newspapers proclaimed the end of an era, the *Daily Times* even going so far as to publish a short list of the "Surviving Pioneers."

I have two mementos of the grandfather I never knew. I bear his name and I carry his gold pocket watch. The latter came to me along with a story that I cherish more than the remarkable timepiece itself. Its back is embossed with three figures—the intertwined initials WJD, a spider, and a wasp. Inside its cover there is photograph of my grandmother, Kathleen McQuillan, herself a daughter of the Comstock, and my Uncle Bud, one of the first children born in Tonopah. Bud's real name was Belmont, which was my grandparents' way of honoring the community of Tonopah's discoverers and, not incidentally, Billy's business partners.

According to the story, the watch was a present from Philadelphia investors who, about 1907, sent their engineers to Nevada to look over potential properties. Billy Douglass had a reputation for grubstaking almost anyone in need, and in the process, he picked up interests in several hundred, mostly worthless, claims throughout the state. He was approached by the eastern engineers and provided them with maps and directions. About a month later, they returned from the desert to make him an offer. It seems that they were prepared to pay $100,000 for the group of claims called the Spider and the Wasp that he held in Wonder (between Fallon and Gabbs). According to Hugh A. Shamberger's recent book on that mining camp, the claims were indeed quite valuable and proved to be among Wonder's best. Billy said he wanted to think it over and would meet with them in the Tonopah Club that evening. There he opined that $100,000 was excessive but that he was willing to sell for $75,000! The deal was made and the buyers commissioned the watch in Switzerland as a token of their appreciation. Is the story true? Possibly.

I believe my grandfather's watch is an excellent example of both the wonderful quality and tenuous nature of Nevada history. It hearkens back to an era long since past but which in so many ways still dominates Nevada thought. It is rather axiomatic that we must learn from history in order to avoid its errors; however, for Nevada's this task is made more difficult because our heritage is as much a creation as a chronicle. Indeed, in at least a psychological sense, one might argue that our historical baseline derives from such works as *Roughing It* and the colorful vignettes from newspapers like the *Territorial Enterprise* and its subsequent mining camp emulators. The image that emerges depicts a world of self-reliant, independent entrepreneurs disposed to extraordinary risk-taking—whether raising livestock in one of the nation's most arid and hostile settings or scratching holes in bleak mountainsides in pursuit of elusive, unlimited wealth. Rather than the product of pioneers seeking to sink roots permanently into virgin soil, the nineteenth-century Nevada settlement comes across as a collectivity more than a community, a group of sojourners of questionable character hoping to make their fortune without breaking too many rules before going elsewhere to spend it. Excepting a few Mormon colonies and the servicing centers that emerged along the transcontinental railway, most Nevada towns were as unstable as the tumbleweeds blowing down Main Street, subject to abandonment and dismantlement at the latest rumor that El Dorado exists and has just been discovered somewhere "over yonder." That the state developed permanent settlement was inevitable, yet viewed from the perspective of nineteenth-century Nevada reality it seems epiphenomenal.

There is a sense in which Nevadans still invoke a spirit of "rugged individualism" anchored in our past. Periodically, it is reaffirmed by our best contemporary writers, as in Robert Laxalt's *Nevada* and his *National Geographic* article "The Other Nevada" or James Hulse's *Forty Years in the Wilderness*. Perhaps this is necessary catharsis for a people who arguably share with Mississippi the dubious distinction of having the worst national image (albeit for different reasons). Yet might we not question whether this provides a viable charter and blueprint for forging our place in the contemporary and future worlds? We were both blessed and cursed by having Mark Twain, one of the consummate writers (and notorious tale spinners) of world literature, among our original interpreters. However, to my mind, Nevadans real challenge lies not in meriting his mastery but in transcending it.

Times Present

I attended Manogue High School when I was a boy growing up in the Reno area—not the present modern school next to the university but the "Old Manogue" quartered in a made-over ranch house situated along the Truckee River southeast of Sparks. Surrounded by miles of pasture, grazing livestock, fruit orchards and fields of vegetables cultivated by Italian truck gardeners, the tiny Catholic high school was truly out in the country. The rural atmosphere was not belied by an urban skyline hovering on the horizon—at least not until the Mapes Hotel was constructed, prompting our awestruck schoolboy imaginations to draw fanciful comparisons with the Empire State Building. Reno and Sparks remained separate communities, linked by old Highway 40, rather than arbitrary divisions on the map of a continuous metropolitan area.

As I reflect back on my high school days, I realize now that I did not so much attend class at the Old Manogue as in the surrounding countryside. A true believer in the anti-intellectualism characteristic of my classmates (pervasive at rival Reno and Sparks high school as well), I found little of interest within the confines of the curriculum. However, I soon discovered the wildlife inhabiting the Truckee River, the farmland sloughs, and the marshes of the nearby Nevada Game Farm. My interest and energy became focused upon the attractions of this magical world and its denizens.

The beginning of the school term meant fur prospecting within walking distance of the high school, as I staked out beaver colonies and muskrat slides and searched for signs of the elusive mink. Late autumn and early winter were devoted to running a trap line that ended at Vista. In the lowering dusk my partner and I would hitchhike back to Reno, entering the vehicles of our unsuspecting benefactors with a wet gunnysack filled with our gear and catch (few dared to ask). In springtime we pursued lizards and snakes, which we marketed by mail to biological supply houses and through our own auspicious sounding "Sierra Reptile Farm."

I gained my literacy during my Manogue years, but not through attentiveness to my teachers. Rather, I became an avid reader of works like Raymond Ditmars's *Reptiles of the World*, trapping and fur farming manuals, and the magazine *Fur-Fish-Game* (to which I contributed my first article—a description of trapping experiences in the Reno area).

Little remains of the world of Old Manogue. The Reno Cannon International Airport and a golf course now occupy the drained marshes of the Nevada Game Farm. A young boy's imagination could scarcely be fired by the asphalt and industrial parks that now cover most of the fields and sloughs that were once my kingdom.

While we were largely unaware of it at the time, the forces that were to convert Nevada into its present reality had already been unleashed. Between 1940 and 1950 the state's population had increased nearly 50 percent, or from 110,000 to 160,000 residents.[1] While northern Nevada experienced some of the growth (Reno gained a third of its 1950 population during the decade), the spectacular development was in Clark County. During the 1950s Washoe County was eclipsed demographically by the upstart to the south; however, for northern Nevadans there was still a qualitative difference between the two. Though only a third of Nevada's population resided in the Reno-Sparks-Carson area, our claim to political and, particularly, intellectual leadership remained unchallenged. Reno, with its 32,000 residents, was the largest city in the state and housed its only university. Carson was the seat of state government. Therefore, we *were* Nevada regardless of what some southern Nevada arrivistes might think. To the extent that we looked elsewhere for spiritual sustenance it was to northern California and "the City," and certainly not to our neighbors in the south with their obvious ties to southern California and "tinsel town." Our smugness might have allowed us alternately to patronize and to ignore the "cow counties" and southerners but, in retrospect, I believe that it was at our peril. For it precluded us from addressing meaningfully Nevada's real twentieth-century challenge—namely, growth and its prerogatives.

In the north, as the growth issue became more and more blatant, we turned against ourselves. Where once there was degree of harmony and community spirit, we divided over such issues as the routing of Interstate 80 and the siting of the convention center and airport. The battles lasted for years and left a legacy of acrimony and bitterness. Suburbanization of commerce, as retail services moved to the shopping centers to be replaced in the downtown area by casino expansion, created new divisions between periphery and core, "residents" and "tourists." In short, public debate in northern Nevada increasingly acquired schizophrenic overtones as we split into "growth" and "no-growth" factions. There was also an element of illogicality and hypocrisy as we became increasingly dependent on the very tourist dollar that we damned and blamed for our environmental problems.

Another source of ambiguity in the public debate was the changing nature of the collective pronoun. With each new census, it became increasingly obvious that "we" referred to a shifting reality. Despite the fumbling attempts to rein in growth, the population of Washoe County almost quadrupled in the three decades between 1950 and 1980 (from 50,000 to 193,000 inhabitants).

Ambivalence best describes my own feelings about the process. I was saddened to watch my old boyhood haunts disappear pell-mell into the irresistible and insatiable maw of development. At the same time, I was pleased to witness the flowering of the arts made possible only by increased population—creation of the Nevada Opera, the Nevada Repertory Theater, the Nevada Festival Ballet, and the Reno Philharmonic, the Sierra Art Museum, and the more than forty other arts organizations that now provide Reno with a variegated cultural landscape. This is in stark contrast with my youth when culture in Reno meant a ticket to the Community Concert Series, to the Reno Little Theater, and to San Francisco. I also cannot ignore the irony when I am exhorted by people who moved to northern Nevada, and thereby changed irreversibly "my" Reno, to make common cause with them against potential newcomers in defense of "our" way of life. How would they have viewed a similar campaign back in the 1950s, when it really might have been possible to opt for a future modeled after Monterey or Ashland? There are disturbing implications for such a process carried to its logical conclusion, for if I have the right to exclude people from Reno, I thereby confer upon someone else the right to exclude me from San Francisco or any other place that I might choose to live.

Meanwhile, the contrast between northern and southern Nevada could not be greater. The combination of disdain and myopia with which we northerners continue to view southerners allows us the delusion that we are still contenders in a contest over the state's economic and political hegemony. For the past four decades northern Nevadans have managed to consistently underestimate the south. For us it seemed axiomatic that the bleak and arid setting of Las Vegas would itself set natural limits upon its capacity for expansion. Who in their right mind would choose to settle permanently in the hottest corner of the continent? Each new Las Vegas project was greeted in the north with incredulity; each cyclical downturn in the southern Nevada economy was treated as a harbinger of imminent collapse. Yet Las Vegas, imbued with a "can do" spirit, not only survived but triumphed beyond the wildest dreams of its sanguine boosters. In the process Clark County acquired nearly 60 percent of the state's population, or approximately two and a half times that of Washoe County.

Consequently, it is no coincidence that today the governor, lieutenant governor, and both of Nevada's U.S. senators are from Clark County. The reapportionment after the 1990 census will further consolidate southern Nevada's political base. In short, the south will enjoy an absolute majority in every statewide political arena. Consequently, Clark County is in a position to dictate Nevada's future social, economic, educational, and political agendas. Indeed, within a democracy is this not as it should be?

At the same time there is a challenge implicit in the new contemporary reality, particularly for northern Nevadans. One questions whether we can afford any longer the luxury of Las Vegas-bashing. I believe that to date southern Nevadans have displayed remarkable restraint in their dealings with the rest of the state. They have yet to flex their political muscle in arbitrary or punitive fashion. There may yet be time to bridge the hundreds of miles, and the even wider conceptual gulf, between the north and the south. One can only conclude that ultimately northern Nevadans have a greater stake in doing so than do our southern Nevada fellow citizens.

Times Future

Mother had a sense of the historic and momentous. When the all but moribund V&T Railroad was about to expire, she took my brother John and me out of school in order to ride the train to Carson City. As the virtually empty car swayed precariously, she lectured two mildly hyper boys, energized by the thrill of sanctioned hooky, on the importance of remembering what struck us as a simple outing.

It was in this same spirit that she awakened us about 4:00 A.M. one brisk autumn morning and bundled us into the car. We drove out of town towards Washoe Valley to escape the lights of the city and parked on a rise facing to the south. Mother made small talk trying to prevent her less than enthusiastic audience from lapsing into slumber. As she voiced her concerns about possible cancellation, the entire horizon exploded in a cold, white flash that lingered momentarily like a fleeting smile on the lips of an oracle and then was gone.

This atomic dawn, telegraphed to us instantaneously from hundreds of miles to the south, left us sobered and speechless. We drove back to Reno through the comforting cloak of restored darkness and stopped for breakfast at an all-night diner. I cannot recall Mother's exact words, but I remember their spirit. Subsequently, I witnessed other detonations from the flanks of Mount Oddie while visiting my cousins in Tonopah. From there we could see the cloud and then feel the tremor. Yet the mood was frivolous and festive as we watched a show that seemingly was staged by the federal government for our benefit in order to countermand the boredom of everyday small-town life. That morning in the diner, however, Mother told us that we had seen the future. It was clear from her demeanor that she was far from pleased.

Father was a gambler in both the figurative and the literal senses of the term. During my youth he was part-owner of a coin-operated device distributorship. Its place of business was on East Second Street, or a short walk from St. Thomas Aquinas grammar school where for a portion of each day I was forced to listen to Dominican nuns naively lecture the *cognoscenti* on the sorrows of purgatory. Once released from daily confinement, however, I could dash down the street to the Nevada Novelty Company and its wonders. There were pinball machines that passed through the premises for repairs before going out "on location" to some bar, restaurant, or bowling alley. If luck was with you, and you managed to be inconspicuous enough not to annoy the adults, you could spend the entire afternoon in an orgy of free games. Of equal interest were the jukeboxes, or rather the used 45 RPM phonograph records that they disgorged. My record collection was never current but it was complete.

The mainstay of the business, of course, was the slot machines. I recall being mystified at the attraction to adults of a device that provided neither interesting sights nor sounds, but I was under no delusion regarding its importance in the grand scheme of things. Indeed, from time to time Father would take me on one of his regular trips to rural Nevada to service his "slot route." We would visit such metropolises as Fallon and Hawthorne, linked by asphalt ribbons, before bouncing over the dirt roads that ended in places like Gabbs and Flanigan. It was there in ramshackle bars or general stores that the Nevada Novelty Company had its three or four slot machines. Usually, at least one would be "out of order" and turned to the wall, awaiting Father's less than polished mechanical skills. As likely as not, it was destined to be our companion in the back of the pickup truck on the trip to the slot-machine hospital in Reno. We would then roll and count the money. With our hand-operated coin wrapper, it took an hour to process even the meager proceeds generated by most locations. When all was ready, the proprietor was first reimbursed for any jackpots paid, after which the remainder was credited to country, state, and federal license fees. Once these expenses were met, the profits were divided fifty-fifty with the proprietor.

As we traveled along the desert tracks, we never discussed his business. It was a time when there were a few small casinos in the north, no Las Vegas strip, Jackpot, or Laughlin. Father was not prone to philosophize. While we counted nickels in back rooms in remote corners of the Nevada desert, it never occurred to him to tell me that I was glimpsing the future, although, of course, I was.

A nation's decision to explode its bombs in Nevada, on the one hand, and counting slot machine proceeds in the heart of the state's mining and ranching district, on the other, encapsulate for me our dilemma as we contemplate the future. That is, for many Nevadans there is a feeling that we are somehow in the clutches of arbitrary outside forces—the federal government and gamblers, each sinister in its own fashion.

Germane to this view is the notion that the authentic Nevada lies somewhere east of Sparks and north of Las Vegas, is rural in character, and resulted when those rugged individualists referred to earlier gained a mining and ranching toehold in a hostile, frontier environment. As a boy I was taught that Nevada was the least populated of the forty-eight states, yet sixth largest in size. In 1940 our 110,000 inhabitants divided niftily into our 110,000 square miles, mathematics which seemed to give each Nevadan a privileged place on the planet, at least as measured in terms of elbow room. While the numbers have changed, the mind-set has not. Psychologically, the state's "wide-open spaces" still constitute for Nevadans a redoubtable refuge in which to escape the crassness of twentieth-century materialism and modernity. More germane to the state's present and future reality, however, is another numerical coincidence. I refer to the fact that if 85 percent of our land, including most of the authentic Nevada, is under federal ownership, as of 1980 85 percent of our population resides in urban centers, largely outside the federal preserve. In terms of percentages, then, and despite our rural imagery, Nevada is the fourth most urbanized state in the nation!

I once lived for a year in Australia and was struck by the similarities between Aussies and Nevadans in this regard. Although a nation of coastal dwellers, of which the overwhelming majority live in five cities, the Australians' national images turn on kangaroos, koala bears, and the Outback. Few Sydney-siders have ever visited the Outback, or plan to, yet concur in the notion that somehow Australia's essence lingers there. As of 1980 approximately 650,000 of Nevada's 800,000 residents lived in the greater Reno and Las Vegas metropolitan areas. As those of us who do frequent Nevada's interior in near solitude can attest, few Renoites or Las Vegans have ever experienced the Black Rock Desert, the Jarbidge county, or Monitor Valley.

Insofar as our rural imagery provides us with psychological strength and satisfaction, it is benign or even positive. However, when it is allowed to assume a critical role in debates over our future, it becomes a legitimate cause for concern. Stripped of their mythic properties, Nevada's ranching and mining traditions seldom proved reliable foundations for the state's economy. In strict ecological terms Nevada has much more in common with Afghanistan than with Iowa and, consequently, its agriculture can be viewed as only marginal at best. Lack of moisture and a short growing season alone set insurmountable limits upon it. This can be contrasted with our mining successes. Indeed, Nevada is one of the most mineral-rich corners of the globe, and individual discoveries such as the Comstock in the mid-nineteenth century, Tonopah-Goldfield at the turn of the century and, more recently, the "invisible" gold operations in places like Carlin provide the state with some of the most spectacular mining booms in the annals of human history. At the same time mining strikes are predicated upon a nonrenewable resource and are, therefore, intrinsically ephemeral.

It is thought provoking to consider the demographics of the state when the economy was based almost exclusively upon ranching and mining. In 1880, or during the afterglow of the Comstock-Austin-Eureka mining discoveries and the homesteading that followed the Civil War, our population reached 62,00 persons. Twenty years later, with the mining industry in a deep depression and agriculture in the doldrums, it had declined by a third to 42,000, and the possibility of stripping Nevada of statehood was under serious consideration by the U.S. Congress. The Tonopah-Goldfield discoveries and their spin-offs essentially saved the day by doubling the state's population to 82,000 by 1910; however, the inevitable playing out of the mines and the vicissitudes of international markets for agricultural and mineral products conspired to reduce our population to 77,000 by the 1920 census.

The essential point is that Nevada's "traditional" economy was incapable of supporting a population of 100,000 inhabitants in the best of times and proved particularly vulnerable to periodic crisis. In its modern guises, it is even less capable of providing a livelihood to our citizenry. By this I mean that nineteenth-century Nevada agriculture and mining were labor intensive compared to their modern counterparts. Last century small family ranches dotted the landscape, multitudes of hard-rock miners worked the diggings, and hundreds of prospectors roamed the desert. Today's ranch incorporates three or four of yesterday's abandoned homesteads, gigantic mining operations employ a few men versed in running state-of-the-art equipment, and a handful of geologists use satellite photos to pinpoint future prospects. Nor, for the most part, are these resources vested in the hands of native rugged individualists. Rather, today's ranch is likely to be owned by a movie star or a physician seeking a tax shelter, and the mines are controlled by multinational corporations.

It is therefore noteworthy that by 1980 rural Nevada's population (defined as everybody outside Washoe and Clark counties) approximates 150,000 persons, or almost twice that of the entire state during the palmier days of ranching and mining. Here, in fact, we confront the real Achilles' heel of the rugged individualist myth, since the bulk of rural Nevadans are employees of either the tourist and gaming industries or the government. Indeed, eliminate the jobs provided by the casinos and motels in Winnemucca, Jackpot, Elko, Wells, Wendover, and Ely; abolish those within the federal, state, and county bureaucracies; and dismiss the civilian employees of Nellis Air Force Base, the Fallon Naval Station, the Hawthorne Munitions Depot, and the Atomic Test Site, as well as those of the civilian defense contractors, and rural Nevada would become a vast economic wasteland. Whimsical "Sagebrush Rebellions" notwithstanding, rural Nevada is one of the most heavily subsidized and economically dependent regions of the nation.

We need only remember the anguished protests of the residents of Austin faced with the transfer of the Lander County seat to Battle Mountain and closure of the local offices of the U.S. National Forest Service, or the decision by Nye County officials to send a lobbyist to Washington, D.C., to argue *for* the national nuclear waste dump (thanks to urban Nevada they got Bullfrog County instead). Conversely, it is a bit ludicrous when Nevada ranchers ask to "get government off our backs." This appeal is by now a litany that is repeated with the same monotony of Tibetan monks spinning their prayer wheels. While it, too, invokes rugged individualism, it ignores the fact that through agricultural price supports and range use fees that are considerably lower than rates on similar private land, the average Nevada rancher is more heavily subsidized than a floor full of welfare mothers in a Detroit housing project.

Such, then, is the past and present reality of the authentic Nevada. By any stretch of the imagination can it inform our future, except by way of a warning? In short, can the approximately one million Nevadans who now call the state home find much that is relevant in this tradition, other than to esteem it for its historical quaintness?

This brings me to the question of Nevada's tourist and gaming economy, frantically promoted in the south while at best tolerated in the north. Many Nevadans view gambling as artificial, a hybrid phenomenon superimposed upon the state by outside interests ranging from the Mafia to Holiday Inns. There is a sense in which this is true, since it can in no way be contended that gaming's spectacular development is a homegrown product. On the other hand, I would argue that the concept is homegrown, and that it is but one manifestation of a broader survival strategy that was honed, beginning about the turn of this century, on the perception that ranching and mining were both fickle paramours. After riding the boom-to-bust roller coaster, which resulted in the demographic fluctuations considered earlier, Nevadans began to posture their state to take advantage of the laws of neighboring ones.

We were the first to legalize prizefighting, and our history as a divorce haven is legendary. When other states liberalized their divorce laws, we invented the quickie marriage, thereby substituting today's wedding chapels for the divorcée dude ranches of my youth. Legalized prostitution and gambling provided additional attractions to potential visitors. A more modern manifestation of the same mentality is the warehouses that banished my muskrats and that offer American industry a legal means of circumventing inventory taxes in California, Oregon, and Washington. Our most recent and possible crowning achievement in shifting our civic responsibilities to others was the tax reform, which essentially insulated us from most of the onus of property tax (we dare not even brook the subject of a state income tax except, as happened in the last election, to banish the possibility through referendum). Thus, we have made our state coffers almost totally reliant upon the tourist trade (through the gaming and sales taxes) and federal rebates. As a consequence, our state government finds it difficult to set any kind of social or educational agenda that requires long-term planning. Rather, state officials are forced to engage in legerdemain with the ledgers, since all budgetary projections remain asterisked, subject to future results in casino counting rooms and merchants' cash registers.

One response to our essential ambivalence regarding near total dependency upon a single industry and its ancillary effects is to heed the clarion call of "economic diversification." While a worthwhile objective, it is fair to question our prospects and, consequently, the role that such aspirations ought to play in planning for the future. Realistically, our new commitment places us squarely in the pack with the forty-nine other states aspiring to host the next Silicon Valley. Without abandoning such initiatives, is it wise to assume in some vague sense that they really will reduce our dependency upon tourism and gaming? At the same time, it may even be relevant to ask whether they should.

By this I mean that, viewed strictly in economic terms, tourism and gaming have provided Nevada with its one unequivocal success story. The state is sometimes referred to as the "Gaming Mecca of the World." Despite the pretentiousness of the statement, it is scarcely hyperbolic since it reflects a certain reality. However, this very fact is a source of considerable ambivalence for some Nevadans.

This is particularly true of northerners who have somehow never quite lived down their shame over the conclusions of the Kefauver Report, which underscored the underworld influence in the state. Each new *Green Felt Jungle*, sensational feature article, or film depicting Nevada in such stereotypic terms only serves to feed the private self-loathing that results from dependence upon a disreputable activity. There are, of course, available defense mechanisms. It is common in the north to draw a distinction between "clean" northern casino operations and "hood"-operated southern ones, an exercise which might have had a certain validity at one time but has now been largely undermined by the progressively corporate nature of casino ownership at both ends of the state. Another ploy is for those who are not involved directly in the industry to maintain the illusion that they are not benefited, and thereby tainted, by it. Hence, some Nevada store clerks, physicians, and professors like to believe that they are insulated from gaming and could continue to pursue their careers here were the industry to simply disappear. Meanwhile, we have produced a cadre of critics, ranging from Cassandras to moralists, who decry the evils of gambling and the precariousness of a society built upon it. While this provides guidance for our self-flagellation and affords catharsis to the guilt-ridden, it also obfuscates many of the real issues as we chart our course.

To my mind, it is essential that we become at least resigned, indeed reconciled, to the future importance of tourism and gambling in the state's economy and image. No one would argue that gambling is a particularly noble enterprise, but neither is it the most ignoble human activity. The salient point is that it appeals to human nature and is therefore a fact of life. Having stated this, however, I would hasten to add that those who believe that Nevada gambling is merely a response to human greed are engaged in gross oversimplification. In such a view, unscrupulous gamblers load the dice against unsuspecting or reckless players blinded by avarice. This is at best a patronizing depiction of the millions of tourists who visit Nevada annually. Indeed, its plausibility is undermined by their sheer numbers. It is also akin to invoking sloth to explain the behavior of the same individuals should they choose to simply lie about on a beach instead.

In reality, Nevada gaming is no longer just about gambling. By this I mean that our resorts now have much more in common with Disneyland, Cannes, Maui, and Acapulco than they do with parlor poker or back-alley dice games. They offer an escape from the mundane by means of what Umberto Eco recently called *Travels in Hyperreality*. It is the Caesar's Palace that somehow eclipses rather than emulates the glories of Ancient Rome— the trip on the Mississippi riverboat without the mosquitoes.

There is a sense in which we have become so accustomed to our internal debate and self-doubts about the worth of the gambling industry that we have ignored its changing image. There was once a time in which virtually all the national press regarding Nevada gaming was negative. Actually, it ranged from voyeuristic to the denigratory. We were essentially regarded as a gambling den and bordello, an aberration within national life. Of late, however, there has been growing recognition that Nevada gambling is actually part of a broader American tradition and that, in terms of architecture and design, it is a path breaker and pacesetter within the world's recreational industry.[2]

Finally, it should be noted that Nevada gaming is no longer unique and, hence, a virtually unchallenged monopoly. There was a time when we were the sole national renegade, at least with respect to casino gambling. This is no longer the case. Legalization of casinos in New Jersey is but the tip of an iceberg. Below the waterline several other states are considering a similar move, and most now have wagering in one form or another. The reality, then, is that Nevada gambling remains preeminent but far from unchallenged. It operates in a national and, increasingly, global market. While we draw some of our visitors from abroad, it is also true that casino gambling has proliferated in the majority of countries on every inhabited continent. In a real sense, we presently compete not just with Atlantic City but with Sun City, not to mention Macao, Monte Carlo, and Montevideo.

The very magnitude of our success, with the attendant per capita income and lifestyle to which we have become accustomed, indeed makes us vulnerable. One need only note the shiver that runs through the body politic at the mention of legalized casino gambling in our prime California market. Such a prospect is by far a greater problem for the state than for Nevada's casinos. The New Jersey experience has demonstrated clearly that expertise within the industry is at a premium. Just as much of the ownership and management of Atlantic City casinos originated in Nevada, should California legalize gaming, it might even prove to be an opportunity for many Nevada gamblers—the same cannot be said of our state. If the casino business transcends Nevada's boundaries and is no longer captive to our enabling legislation, as a state we have entered upon a new era of dependency upon it, at least until such time as we develop a viable alternative. This dependency is increasingly like that of Youngstown upon the steel industry. Steel plants can be relocated, Youngstown cannot. Consequently, we might question the utility of incessant hand wringing over what may be our ineluctable economic destiny.

Mirrors and Masks

Despite the critical tone in much of this essay, it is not my purpose to be peevish or pontifical. Indeed, I declare unabashedly that I love Nevada. In addition to being a native son, I am a returned native, since I now reside here by choice after having lived in many other parts of America and the world. In criticizing that which is so much a part of me, I feel like the proud parent who seeks to appreciate the virtues without being blinded to the faults of his beautiful, yet troublesome child.

There is a sense in which the analogy is particularly appropriate, since Nevada may be regarded as an adolescent. By this I meant that our recent growth is like that of the teenager whose physical maturity suddenly begins to far outstrip his emotional development. As a state our appearance has assumed adult form, yet we continue to have private doubts and fears regarding our future career. Given the fact that we have increased our population tenfold in less than half a century, it is scarcely surprising that we suffer at this point in our history from what might be likened to raging hormonal imbalance.

The only "cure" for adolescent woes is the progressive development of a self-concept and hence self-confidence. In successfully forging an adult *persona*, the individual contemplates his childhood, largely in order to become reconciled with its passing, and assesses his present circumstances, in order to be realistic about his prospects. In this regard, both the past and present become the mirrors in which he learns about himself in order to shed the masks of youth in favor of assuming an adult role. Collectively, we Nevadans face a similar challenge. It is the purpose of this essay to suggest that it is only possible to transcend our adolescence if we are willing to remove our mask *before* gazing into our mirrors.

Notes

1 All the population figures cited in this essay were adapted by rounding off the statistics provided in *Population Abstract of the United States, Volume One, Tables*, ed. John L. Androit (McLean, Virginia: Androit Associates, 1983), 502–505.

2 Cf. John M. Findlay, *People of Chance: Gambling in American Society from Jamestown to Las Vegas* (New York: Oxford University Press, 1986) and Robert Venturi, Denise Scott Brown, and Steven Izenour, *Learning From Las Vegas* (Cambridge: The MIT Press, 1972).

"Las Vegas (What?) Las Vegas (Can't Hear You! Too Noisy) Las Vegas!!!!"
(1965)

Tom Wolfe

*There have been more than 1000 major articles published since 1940 that describe the city of Las Vegas. Beginning with "Wild, Wooly, and Wide-Open," (*Look*, August, 1940), down to a cover story in* Time *Magazine in 1994, Americans have never lost their fascination for Las Vegas. One of the most important of these many essays was published in 1964 in* Esquire *by the* avant garde *journalist Tom Wolfe. This essay provided him entre into a non-traditional examination of American culture during the 1960s that appeared in his controversial book,* The Kandy Kolored Tangerine-Flake Streamline Baby *(1965). In Las Vegas, Wolfe discovered a "super-hyperversion" of what he proclaimed to be America's emerging "new style of life."*

. . . Raymond, who is thirty-four years old and works as an engineer in Phoenix, is big but not terrifying. He has the sort of thatchwork hair that grows so low all along the forehead there is no logical place to part it, but he tries anyway. He has a huge, prognathous jaw, but it is as smooth, soft and round as a melon, so that Raymond's total effect is that of an Episcopal divinity student.

The guards were wonderful. They were dressed in cowboy uniforms like Bruce Cabot in *Sundown* and they wore sheriff's stars.

"Mister, is there something we can do for you?"

"The expression is 'Sir,'" said Raymond. "You said 'Mister.' The expression is 'Sir.' How's your old Cosa Nostra?"

Amazingly, the casino guards were easing Raymond out peaceably, without putting a hand on him. I had never seen the fellow before, but possibly because I had been following his progress for the last five minutes, he turned to me and said, "Hey, do you have a car? This wild stuff is starting again."

The gist of it was that he had left his car somewhere and he wanted to ride up the Strip to the Stardust, one of the big hotel-casinos. I am describing this big goof Raymond not because he is a typical Las Vegas tourist, although he has some typical symptoms, but because he is a good example of the marvelous impact Las Vegas has on the senses. Raymond's senses were at a high pitch of excitation, the only trouble being that he was going off his nut. He had been up since Thursday afternoon, and it was now about 3:45 A.M. Sunday. He had an envelope full of pep pills—amphetamine—in his left coat pocket and an envelope full of Equanils—meprobamate—in his right pocket, or were the Equanils in the left and the pep pills in the right? He could tell by looking but he wasn't going to look anymore. He didn't care to see how many were left.

He had been rolling up and down the incredible electric-sign gauntlet of Las Vegas' Strip, U.S. Route 91, where the neon and the par lamps—bubbling, spiraling, rocketing, and exploding in sunbursts ten stories high out in the middle of the desert—celebrate one-story casinos. He had been gambling and drinking and eating now and again at the buffet tables the casinos keep heaped with food day and night, but mostly hopping himself up with good old amphetamine, cooling himself down with meprobamate, then hooking down more alcohol, until now, after sixty hours, he was slipping into the symptoms of toxic schizophrenia.

He was also enjoying what the prophets of hallucinogen call "consciousness expansion." The man was psychedelic. He was beginning to isolate the components of Las Vegas' unique bombardment of the senses. He was quite right about this *hernia hernia* stuff. Every casino in Las Vegas is, among the other things, a room full of craps tables with dealers who keep up a running singsong that sounds as though they are saying "hernia, hernia, hernia, hernia, hernia" and so on. There they are day and night, easing a running commentary through their nostrils. What they have to say contains next to no useful instruction. Its underlying message is, We are the initiates, riding the crest of chance. That the accumulated sound comes out "hernia" is merely an unfortunate phonetic coincidence. Actually, it is part of something rare and rather grand: a combination of baroque stimuli that brings to mind the bronze gongs, no larger than a blue plate, that Louis XIV, his ruff collars larded with the lint of the foul Old City of Byzantium, personally hunted out in the bazaars of Asia Minor to provide exotic acoustics for his new palace outside Paris.

The sounds of the craps dealer will be in, let's say, the middle register. In the lower register will be the sound of the old babes at the slot machines. Men play the slots too, of course, but one of the indelible images of Las Vegas is that of the old babes at the row upon row of slot machines. There they are at six o'clock Sunday morning no less than at three o'clock Tuesday afternoon. Some of them pack their old hummocky shanks into Capri pants, but many of them just put on the old print dress, the same one day after day, and the old hob-heeled shoes, looking like they might be going out to buy eggs in Tupelo, Mississippi. They have a Dixie Cup full of nickles or dimes in the left hand and an Iron Boy work glove on the right hand to keep the calluses from getting sore. Every time they pull the handle, the machine makes a sound much like the sound a cash register makes before the bell rings, then the slot pictures start clattering up from left to right, the oranges, lemons, plums, cherries, bells, bars, buckaroos—the figure of a cowboy riding a bucking bronco. The whole sound keeps churning up over and over again in eccentric series all over the place, like one of those random-sound radio symphonies by John Cage. You can hear it at any hour of the day or night all over Las Vegas. You can walk down Fremont Street at dawn and hear it without even walking in a door, that and the spins of the wheels of fortune, a boring and not very popular sort of simplified roulette, as the tabs flap to a stop. As an overtone, or at times simply as a loud sound, comes the babble of the casino crowds, with an occasional shriek from the craps tables, or, anywhere from 4 P.M. to 6 A.M., the sound of brass instruments or electrified string instruments from the cocktail-lounge shows.

The crowd and band sounds are not very extraordinary, of course. But Las Vegas' Muzak is. Muzak pervades Las Vegas from the time you walk into the airport upon landing to the last time you leave the casinos. It is piped out to the swimming pool. It is in the drugstores. It is as if there were a communal fear that someone, somewhere in Las Vegas, was going to be left with a totally vacant minute on his hands.

Las Vegas has succeeded in wiring an entire city with this electronic stimulation, day and night, out in the middle of the desert. In the automobile I rented, the radio could not be turned off, no matter which dial you went after. I drove for days in a happy burble of Action Checkpoint News, "Monkey No. 9," "Donna, Donna, the Prima Donna," and picking-and-singing jingles for the Frontier Bank and the Fremont Hotel.

One can see the magnitude of the achievement. Las Vegas takes what in other American towns is but a quixotic inflammation of the senses for some poor salary mule in the brief interval between the flagstone rambler and the automatic elevator downtown and magnifies it, foliates it, embellishes it into an institution.

For example, Las Vegas is the only town in the world whose skyline is made up neither of buildings, like New York, nor of trees, like Wilbraham, Massachusetts, but signs. One can look at Las Vegas from a mile away on Route 91 and see no buildings, no trees, only signs. But such signs! They tower. They revolve, they oscillate, they soar in shapes before which the existing vocabulary of art history is helpless. I can only attempt to supply names—Boomerang Modern, Palette Curvilinear, Flash Gordon Ming-Alert Spiral, McDonald's Hamburger Parabola, Mint Casino Elliptical, Miami Beach Kidney. Las Vegas' sign makers work so far out beyond the frontiers of conventional studio art that they have no names themselves for the forms they create. Vaughan Cannon, one of those tall blond Westerners, the builders of places like Las Vegas and Los Angeles, whose eyes seem to have been bleached by the sun, is in the back shop of the Young Electric Sign Company out on East Charleston Boulevard with Herman Boernge, one of his designers, looking at the model they have prepared for the Lucky Strike Casino sign, and Cannon points to where the sign's two great curving faces meet to form a narrow vertical face and says:

"Well, here we are again—what do we call that?"

"I don't know," says Boernge. "It's sort of a nose effect. Call it a nose."

Okay, a nose, but it rises sixteen stories high above a two-story building. In Las Vegas no farseeing entrepreneur buys a sign to fit a building he owns. He rebuilds the building to support the biggest sign he can get up the money for and, if necessary, changes the name. The Lucky Strike Casino today is the Lucky Casino, which fits better when recorded in sixteen stories of flaming peach and incandescent yellow in the middle of the Mojave Desert. In the Young Electric Sign Co. era signs have become the architecture of Las Vegas, and the most whimsical, Yale-seminar-frenzied devices of the two late geniuses of Baroque Modern, Frank Lloyd Wright and Eero Saarinen, seem rather stuffy business, like a jest at a faculty meeting, compared to it. Men like Boernge, Kermit Wayne, Ben Mitchem and Jack Larsen, formerly an artist for Walt Disney, are the designer-sculptor geniuses of Las Vegas, but their motifs have been carried faithfully throughout the town by lesser men, for gasoline stations, motels, funeral parlors, churches, public buildings, flophouses and sauna baths.

Then there is a stimulus that is both visual and sexual—the Las Vegas buttocks décolletage. This is a form of sexually provocative dress seen more and more in the United States, but avoided like Broadway message-embroidered ("Kiss Me, I'm Cold") underwear in the fashion pages, so that the euphemisms have not been established and I have no choice but clinical terms. To achieve buttocks décolletage a woman wears bikini-style shorts that cut across the round fatty masses of the buttocks rather than cupping them from below, so that the outer-lower edges of these fatty masses, or "cheeks," are exposed. I am in the cocktail lounge of the Hacienda Hotel, talking to managing director Dick Taylor about the great success his place has had in attracting family and tour groups, and all around me the waitresses are bobbing on their high heels, bare legs and décolletage-bare backsides, set off by pelvis-length lingerie of an uncertain denomination. I stare, but I am new here. At the White Cross Rexall drugstore on the Strip a pregnant brunette walks in off the street wearing black shorts with buttocks décolletage aft and illusion-of-cloth nylon lingerie hanging fore, and not even the old mom's-pie pensioners up near the door are staring. They just crank away at the slot machines. On the streets of Las Vegas, not only the show girls, of which the town has about two hundred fifty, bona fide, in residence, but girls of every sort, including, especially, Las Vegas' little high-school buds, who adorn what locals seeking roots in the sand call "our city of churches and schools," have taken up the chic of wearing buttocks décolletage step-ins under flesh-tight slacks, with the outline of the undergarment showing through fashionably. Others go them one better. They achieve the effect of having been dipped once, briefly, in Helenca stretch nylon. More and more they look like those wonderful old girls out of Flash Gordon who were wrapped just once over in Baghdad pantaloons of clear polyethylene with only Flash Gordon between them and the insane red-eyed assaults of the minions of Ming. It is as if all the hip young suburban gals of America named Lana, Deborah and Sandra, who gather wherever the arc lights shine and the studs steady their coiffures in the plate-glass reflection, have convened in Las Vegas with their bouffant hair above and anatomically stretch-pant-swathed little bottoms below, here on the new American frontier. But exactly!

None of it would have been possible, however, without one of those historic combinations of nature and art that creates an epoch. In this case, the Mojave Desert plus the father of Las Vegas, the late Benjamin "Bugsy" Siegel.

Bugsy was an inspired man. Back in 1944 the city fathers of Las Vegas, their Protestant rectitude alloyed only by the giddy prospect of gambling revenues, were considering the sort of ordinance that would have preserved the town with a kind of Colonial Williamsburg dinkiness in the motif of the Wild West. All new buildings would have to have at least the façade of the sort of place where piano players used to wear garters on their sleeves in Virginia City around 1880. In Las Vegas in 1944, it should be noted, there was nothing more stimulating in the entire town than a Fremont Street bar where the composer of "Deep in the Heart of Texas" held forth and the regulars downed fifteen-cent beer.

Bugsy pulled into Las Vegas in 1945 with several million dollars that, after his assassination, was traced back in the general direction of gangster-financiers. Siegel put up a hotel-casino such as Las Vegas had never seen and called it the Flamingo—all Miami Modern, and the hell with piano players with garters and whatever that was all about. Everybody drove out Route 91 just to gape. Such shapes! Boomerang Modern supports, Palette Curvilinear bars, Hot Shoppe Cantilever roofs and a scalloped swimming pool. Such colors! All the new electrochemical pastels of the Florida littoral: tangerine, broiling magenta, livid pink, incarnadine, fuchsia demure, Congo ruby, methyl green, viridine, aquamarine, phenosafranine, incandescent orange, scarlet-fever purple, cyanic blue, tessellated bronze, hospital-fruit-basket orange. And such signs! Two cylinders rose at either end of the Flamingo—eight stories high and covered from top to bottom with neon rings in the shape of bubbles that fizzed all eight stories up into the desert sky all night long like an illuminated whisky-soda tumbler filled to the brim with pink champagne.

The business history of the Flamingo, on the other hand, was not such a smashing success. For one thing, the gambling operation was losing money at a rate that rather gloriously refuted all the recorded odds of the gaming science. Siegel's backers apparently suspected that he was playing both ends against the middle in collusion with professional gamblers who hung out at the Flamingo as though they had liens on it. What with one thing and another, someone decided by the night of June 20, 1947, that Benny Siegel, lord of the Flamingo, had had it. He was shot to death in Los Angeles.

Yet Siegel's aesthetic, psychological and cultural insights, like Cézanne's, Freud's and Max Weber's, could not die. The Siegel vision and the Siegel aesthetic were already sweeping Las Vegas like gold fever. And there were builders of the West equal to the opportunity. All over Las Vegas the incredible electric pastels were repeated. Overnight the Baroque Modern forms made Las Vegas one of the few architecturally unified cities of the world— the style was Late American Rich—and without the bother and bad humor of a City Council ordinance. No enterprise was too small, too pedestrian or too solemn for The Look. The Supersonic Carwash, the Mercury Jetaway, Gas Vegas Village and Terrible Herbst gasoline stations, the Par-a-Dice Motel, the Palm Mortuary, the Orbit Inn, the Desert Moon, the Blue Onion Drive-In—on it went, like Wildwood, New Jersey, entering Heaven.

The atmosphere of the six-mile-long Strip of hotel-casinos grips even those segments of the population who rarely go near it. Barely twenty-five-hundred feet off the Strip, over by the Convention Center, stands Landmark Towers, a shaft thirty stories high, full of apartments, supporting a huge circular structure shaped like a space observation platform, which was to have contained the restaurant and casino. Somewhere along the way Landmark Towers went bankrupt, probably at that point in the last of the many crises when the construction workers *still* insisted on spending half the day flat on their bellies with their heads, tongues and eyeballs hanging over the edge of the tower, looking down into the swimming pool of the Playboy Apartments below, which has a "nudes only" section for show girls whose work calls for a tan all over.

Elsewhere, Las Vegas' beautiful little high-school buds in their buttocks-décolletage stretch pants are back on the foam-rubber upholstery of luxury broughams peeling off the entire chick ensemble long enough to establish the highest venereal-disease rate among high-school students anywhere north of the yaws-rotting shanty jungles of the Eighth Parallel. The Negroes who have done much of the construction work in Las Vegas' sixteen-year boom are off in their ghetto on the west side of town, and some of them are smoking marijuana, eating peyote buttons and taking horse (heroin), which they get from Tijuana, I mean it's simple, baby, right through the mails, and old Raymond, the Phoenix engineer, does not have the high life to himself. . . .

"A-Bombs in the Backyard: Southern Nevada Adapts to the Nuclear Age, 1951–1963"
(1983)

A. Costandina Titus

In 1980, Nevadans of all political persuasions and geographical location overwhelmingly opposed establishment of the massive MX mobile missile deployment system being advocated by military planners. This marked the first time Nevadans had resisted the expenditure of large sums of federal dollars within the State. Later Nevadans came together again to fight the use of Yucca Mountain as the national repository for nuclear waste. These two strong protests, however, contrast sharply with the reaction of Nevadans in 1951 when the Federal Government established the Nevada Test Site and began testing nuclear weapons above ground. Nevada's reaction to becoming the host for nuclear tests—and thereby becoming an important part of the Cold War—is explored by A. Costandina Titus, a Professor of Political Science at the University of Nevada, Las Vegas.

> . . . There have been so many detonations of nuclear devices at the test site in the past
> ten years that the community [of Las Vegas] is completely accustomed to, and un-
> concerned about, radiation hazards from such operations.[1]

Nineteen eighty-three marks the twentieth year since mushroom clouds last appeared above the Nevada desert. On August 5, 1963, the Limited Test Ban Treaty was signed, moving atomic weapons testing underground and ending an era of great significance in American and Nevada history. This essay examines the years of atmospheric testing, 1951 to 1963, and two main themes are emphasized. First, it describes the government's atomic testing policy with emphasis on activities at the Nevada Test Site (NTS) and the Atomic Energy Committee's public relations program designed to win popular support for these "backyard" operations. Second, the essay analyzes Southern Nevada's response to the atmospheric testing program by examining the politics, the press, and the popular culture of the region during those years. The inescapable conclusion of this inquiry is that throughout the dozen years of above-ground testing, Nevadans enthusiastically supported the atomic testing program and considered the NTS an asset to the state's development.

Historical Background

At 5:30 a.m. on July 16, 1945, the United States exploded "Trinity," the world's first atomic bomb, at White Sands near Alamogordo, New Mexico. The secretive work of the Manhattan Project was declared a success.[2] President Truman, conferring in Potsdam at the time with Churchill and Stalin, was immediately notified that ". . . results seem satisfactory and already exceed expectations."[3] Within two weeks similar bombs were dropped on Japan, devastating two of its cities and bringing World War II to a close.

Although it was the first nation to develop the A-bomb, the United States had little understanding of the future potential force and effects of such a weapon. To acquire that knowledge, the Joint Chiefs of Staff, shortly after the end of the war, ordered a task force to select "a suitable site which [would] permit accomplishment of atomic tests with acceptable risks and minimum hazards."[4] Such a site had to meet several requirements: it had to be in an area under U.S. control and in a suitable climatic zone; it had to be uninhabited or sparsely populated; and, of course, it had to be far away from the United States.[5]

In January 1946, the government selected as the best site Bikini Atoll, a semicircular chain of some thirty small land dots located in the Marshall Islands region of Micronesia, 2,400 miles southwest of Hawaii.[6] On February 10, 1946, Commander Ben Wyatt, military governor of the Marshalls, addressed the residents of the atoll and told them they would have to move. He compared the Bikinians to the children of Israel whom the Lord had saved from their enemy and led into the Promised Land. "Would you be willing to sacrifice your island for the welfare of all men?" he asked.[7] The Bikinians agreed to move, and they were relocated that spring on Rongerik Atoll; the government promised to take care of them there until it was safe to return.[8]

"Operation Crossroads" began immediately. This first series of tests consisted of two shots, "Test Able," detonated on July 1 in the air over a target fleet including the venerable battleship *Nevada*, and "Test Baker" on July 25, an underwater explosion designed to test the effects of a nuclear blast on the hulls of ocean vessels and submarines. These shots received international press coverage; for the first time, reporters from every major American and European newspaper and magazine witnessed and described a nuclear explosion.[9] By

1958, when President Eisenhower ended the South Pacific testing program, twenty-three nuclear devices, including the hydrogen bomb, had been detonated on Bikini.[10]

Meanwhile, a second atomic testing site was established in the fall of 1947 at nearby Eniwetok Atoll, where forty-three tests were to be conducted over the next ten years.[11] Again people were relocated and the island was closed for security reasons. The first tests conducted at the new site were dubbed "Operation Sandstone," and they resembled the Bikini maneuvers in both the nature of the bombs detonated and the experiments conducted. One major difference existed, however: whereas "Crossroads" was witnessed by the international press, the "Sandstone" series occurred under a virtual news blackout. Secrecy was the order of the day; posters depicting a fish with his mouth open warned participants, "Don't be a sucker. Keep your mouth shut."[12]

Atomic Testing in Nevada

While tests were being conducted in the South Pacific, pressure was building for a site within the continental United States. The creation of such an installation would simplify the complex logistical problems and reduce the mounting costs of managing, supplying, and safeguarding a remote test area. Prompted by the Soviet detonation of an atomic bomb in August 1949[13] and U.S. involvement in the Korean conflict, the ARC[14] ignored persistent warnings from the scientific community about possible health hazards and appealed to President Truman to establish such a continental test site. Relying on a top secret feasibility study code-named "Nutmeg" conducted three years earlier by the Pentagon, the AEC further recommended that the site be located at the Las Vegas-Tonopah Bombing and Gunnery Range which was situated in the desert of Nye County some sixty-five miles northwest of Las Vegas.[15]

The southern Nevada site was selected from a list of five possibilities which included Alamogordo/White Sands, New Mexico; Dugway Proving Ground, Utah; Pamlico Sound/ Camp Lejuene, North Carolina; and a fifty-mile-wide strip between Fallon and Eureka, Nevada. The AEC chose the site near Las Vegas for reasons similar to those used in the selection of Bikini and Eniwetok: it was the largest area; it was already under complete control of the federal government; it enjoyed little rainfall and predictable winds from the west; and it had a very low population density. Furthermore, it was a site whose security could not easily be impaired by an outside enemy force; and Camp Mercury, the temporary air base located at the tip of the 5,400 square mile gunnery range, could readily be converted into a testing center.[16]

On December 18, 1950, President Truman approved the opening of the Nevada site; and six weeks later, on January 27, 1951, the first atmospheric test was conducted over a section of the desert known as Frenchman's Flat. This initial series, "Operation Ranger," consisted of five bombs, dropped from the air, which ranged from one to twenty-two kilotons in yield. The shots were fairly uneventful with the exception of the fourth, an eight kiloton device detonated on February 2, which shattered several store windows in Las Vegas and prompted one scientist to report that "the factors controlling this are poorly understood."[17] Safety monitors detected no "significant levels" of radioactivity outside the testing area, and no one received any detectable injuries during the series. All in all, the operation was praised for its efficiency, safety, and speed.[18]

Plans were immediately made for the expansion of facilities at the test site. Eight million dollars were appropriated and construction was begun on utility and operational structures, including a communication system, a control area, several detonating towers, and additional personnel accommodations. As a safety measure, ground zero (the point of detonation) was moved twenty miles north from Frenchman's Flat to Yucca Flat, a huge expanse of desert surrounded on all sides by mountains.[19] And even more significantly, arrangements were made between the AEC and the military for soldiers to participate in atomic warfare maneuvers at ground zero, beginning with the next test series scheduled for October. These exercises were to provide tactical training for the troops and allow researchers to observe and evaluate the psychological impact of the bomb on participants. To accommodate these needs Camp Desert Rock was built to station troops near the test site.[20]

From 1951 through 1958, the NTS was the location of 119 atmospheric tests of nuclear devices. Thirty-one of those were safety experiments which produced very slight or no nuclear yield. Twelve of these 31 were conducted at the surface; six in tunnels; seven in uncased and unstemmed holes; five from the top of steel or wooden towers; and 1 suspended from a balloon. In addition, there were 88 weapons-related tests which did produce a nuclear explosion; these included one at the surface; one rocket; one airburst fired from a 280mm cannon; two cratering experiments; five in tunnels; 19 dropped from aircraft; 23 suspended from balloons; and 36 from the tops of steel or wooden towers.[21]

There was a short-lived, voluntary moratorium on nuclear testing, agreed to by the U.S. and the U.S.S.R., between October 1958 and August 1961. Upon its expiration, testing resumed and there were 102 American detonations occurring over the next two-year period. Of these, however, all but five were deep, underground shots; one of the five was a cratering test and the other four were at or near the surface.[22] When the Limited Test Ban Treaty (prohibiting testing in outer space, underwater, or in the atmosphere) was signed in Moscow on August 5, 1963, atomic testing moved underground, and some 400 shots have been fired to date.[23]

Selling the Bomb at Home

The 1950 decision to begin atomic testing within the continental United States was made in great secrecy and with extreme caution. In his memoirs, President Truman recalled the need to take special care not to frighten people about "shooting off bombs in their backyards."[24] From the start, every effort was made by the federal government to insure not only public acceptance but also support for the new "backyard" testing program.

First and foremost, the government took the position that the continued development of nuclear weapons was absolutely essential to the country's national security. In light of international developments after World War II,[25] it was not difficult to convince the public that the communists were a distinct threat to the American way of life. Loyalty oaths for government employees were required;[26] the House Un-American Activities Committee investigated dozens of people;[27] and the Rosenbergs were executed as atomic spies.[28] Such red-scare tactics were reinforced by the preparedness activities of the Federal Civil Defense Administration, an agency created by Congress in December 1950 to establish community bomb shelters and instruct the public on how to protect itself in the event of a nuclear attack.[29] The military also propagated the notion of a potential nuclear war with the Soviets; soldiers at Camp Desert Rock participated in mock battles against an enemy which was always portrayed as a communist force invading the U.S.[30]

The government's second strategy for gaining popular acceptance of the testing program was to constantly assure the people that the tests were safe. Numerous proclamations were issued by the AEC throughout the decade of the 1950s claiming that radioactive fall-out posed no danger to human health.[31] In addition, 30,000 copies of a small green pamphlet entitled "Atomic Tests in Nevada" were distributed locally to convince the neighbors of the test site that the blasts were benign. The pamphlet began by apologizing to the residents in the case they had been "inconvenienced" by the operations, and went on to claim that ". . . findings have confirmed that Nevada test fallout has not caused illness or injured the health of anyone living near the test site."[32] It contained cartoons and rhetoric which made light of the potential danger of fallout from the tests; the precautionary measures which residents were advised to take suggested that the risks were minimal: "Your best action is not to be worried about fallout."[33]

Evidence contrary to this position was suppressed or discredited. In the spring of 1953 when some 3,400 sheep, grazing near the test site, died after being exposed to radioactive fallout, the AEC reported that "the highest radiation dosage to the thyroid [of the sheep] has been calculated to be far below the quantity necessary to produce detectable injury."[34] And on March 1, 1954, following the "Bravo" H-bomb shot, when the wind shifted and carried radioactive fallout over several inhabited islands[35] and a Japanese tuna fishing boat,[36] AEC Chairman Lewis Strauss reported to the press, "Today, a full month after the event, the medical staff . . . advised us that they anticipate no illness, barring of course disease which might be hereafter contracted."[37]

Third, the government argued that continued testing was vitally needed for the development of peaceful uses of atomic energy.[38] As early as 1948, the testing at Eniwetok was justified not only on grounds of national security, but also because it would "yield valuable information pertaining to the civilian employment of atomic energy."[39] This was to become a familiar rationalization in the years to come. For instance, when testing began to move underground in 1957, it was declared that such experiments would augment the development of mining and natural gas production.[40] And in 1962 the "Plowshare Program" was initiated; drawing its name from the Biblical verse in Isaiah, "when men shall beat their swords into plowshares," the program involved testing of nuclear devices for such civilian uses as digging harbors or canals, developing underground water supplies, and opening new reserves of oil.[41]

Throughout this entire period the government was also involved in a general public relations campaign to promote a positive view of atomic power in all its forms. Various public relations techniques, including films, brochures, traveling exhibits, science fairs, public speakers, and classroom demonstrations, were employed.[42] The AEC even helped the Boy Scouts create an atomic energy merit badge;[43] and the American Museum of Atomic Energy was opened in Oak Ridge, Tennessee.[44] No stone was left unturned as the government sought to sell the bomb to the American people.

Public Response

These various propagandistic efforts by the U.S. government were overwhelmingly successful. Throughout the fifties and early sixties the vast majority of citizens strongly supported further development and stockpiling of nuclear weapons, and implicitly endorsed continued testing in Nevada. Those few who did not were routinely accused of ignorance, hysteria, or involvement in communist plots.[45]

The most vocal opponents of atmospheric testing during these years were scientists who expressed growing concern over cumulative fallout effects. Among their ranks were such noted researchers as Stanley Livingston, President of the Federation of American Scientists; Hermann Muller, Nobel prize winner in genetics; George Beadle, President of the American Association for the Advancement of Science; and Linus Pauling, winner of Nobel prizes in chemistry and peace. For several years a scientific debate raged between these men and the AEC over the possible long-term effects of exposure to radioactive fallout.[46]

The press, however, gave only limited coverage to these scientists who challenged the wisdom of continued testing; consequently, the issue did not become a public one until the 1956 Presidential election. That summer the dangers of fallout were televised nationwide from the Democratic National Convention, and Adlai Stevenson began his campaign with a promise to halt H-bomb tests. Despite considerable evidence presented on the genetic and strontium 90 hazards from the tests, the country (including Nevada) went strongly for incumbent Eisenhower, a longtime proponent of the testing program.[47]

By the late 1950s, with red-baiting on the wane, the anti-testing movement picked up a little momentum. The National Committee for a Sane Nuclear Policy was founded in November 1957, and within one year had recruited 25,000 members.[48] Small scale "Ban the Bomb" protests took the form of sit-ins at missile bases and refusals to participate in air-raid drills.[49] More dramatic incidents involved several attempts by activists to sail into the Marshall Islands testing zone.[50] Nonetheless, the prevailing view remained steadfastly supportive of the government's position throughout the Cold War era.

Response in Nevada

Support for the atmospheric testing program exhibited by the majority of people in the United States was even greater among the citizens of Nevada.[51] When the government first announced the testing was to be conducted in Southern Nevada, the locals welcomed the infusion of funds that a testing facility would generate. Las Vegas had a limited economy and small population base, and the federal expenditure of millions of dollars and the establishment of a permanent payroll meant increased financial prosperity. Employment opportunities increased; real estate prices rose; and the construction industry boomed. Scores of professional scientists were attracted to the area; and Las Vegas suppliers of varied goods and services enjoyed a bonanza. Even the budding tourist business flourished as people flocked to Las Vegas not just to gamble but to see the mushroom clouds and watch history in the making. As a result, most Nevadans during the fifties seemed generally to believe that the economic advantages of the AEC operations in the state outweighed any potential dangers.[52]

This positive attitude toward the atomic testing program in Nevada was evident on three levels. First, the powerful politicians of the state supported the AEC's activities both in Washington and in Carson City. Second, local newspaper coverage of the test site operations during these years was consistently favorable. And finally, the mushroom cloud itself became a prevalent symbol of southern Nevada's popular culture.

In 1950 Nevada was represented in the U.S. Senate by a powerful Democrat, Patrick A. McCarran.[53] Realizing McCarran's potential influence as a member of the Senate Appropriations Committee, AEC Chairman Gordon Dean paid him a special, personal visit to inform him of plans to open the NTS before it was publicly announced. This "courting" continued to insure McCarran's support and smooth the way for AEC activities in his state.[54] It worked. McCarran consistently voted for increased funding for the AEC, praising the agency for its precision and care in making its tests: "The lead in development of this science is in the best interest of the United States, and we must maintain it. We have an avowed enemy who is developing atomic energy and we must keep ahead."[55]

Nevada's governor during the early fifties, Charles Russell, also publicly defended the NTS against any criticism which arose from leery constituents. His attitude toward the testing activities was captured by his comment to a *New Yorker* reporter in 1952: "We had long ago written off that terrain as wasteland and today it's blooming with atoms."[56] . . .

This stand taken by the local papers was hardly surprising. From the start, news coverage of the testing program was presented in optimistic terms: "Baby A-Blast May Provide Facts on Defense Against Atomic Attack,"[63] "Use of Taller Towers . . . Introduces an Added Angle of Safety . . .,"[64] and "Fallout on Las Vegas and Vicinity . . . Very Low and Without Any Effects on Health."[65] Editorials invariably took the AEC's side. On January 15, 1951, just prior to the first test blast conducted at the NTS, the *Review Journal* reassured its readers that the furor regarding A-bombs at Indian Springs was "entirely uncalled for."[66] Shortly thereafter, on January 30, 1951, the *Sun* stated "atomic experimentation must be carried on if we are to maintain our lead in the atomic and guided missiles field."[67] In the spring of 1953, following the "Dirty Harry" shot which sprinkled fallout on St. George, when Utah Representative Stringfellow called for an end to testing in Nevada, the *Review Journal* warned Stringfellow to stay out of Nevada's business and editorialized, "We like the AEC. We welcome them to Nevada for their tests because we, as patriotic Americans, believe we are contributing something in our small way, to the protection of the land we love."[68]

Local reporters frequently traveled the sixty-five miles to Camp Mercury to cover the announced test blasts. Perched on bleachers at News Nob ten miles from ground zero, they witnessed, photographed, and reported on the nuclear detonations. It was deemed a privilege to be a member of the Ancient and Honorable Society of Bomb Watchers, which included Walter Cronkite, Dave Galloway, John Cameron Swayze, and Bob Considine among its members.[69] Hardly a day passed during the fifties and early sixties when some story dealing with atomic weapons or a related topic did not appear on the front page.

One particularly noteworthy story revolved around the "Shamrock" shot on March 17, 1953. A typical American community was constructed near ground zero to determine what would happen if it were to become the target of an enemy's atomic bomb. Officially named "Survival City," it was soon dubbed "Doom Town" by troops and reporters. The houses were fully furnished and stocked with supplies, and late model cars were parked in garages; mannequins wearing the latest fashions represented inhabitants of all ages.[70]

Graphically describing the aftermath of a similar exercise, Archie Teague of the *Review Journal* wrote, "Potshot inspection tours were held to learn the odds of survival in the atomic age. People played by dummies lay dead and dying in basements, living rooms, kitchens, and bedrooms."[71] Such accounts were typical of the coverage during these shots; they focused on the descriptive, visual implications of the bomb and failed to question more serious potential hazards.

Not only did atomic news dominate the headlines, but the mushroom cloud also became the symbol of the generation, quickly permeating many aspects of the local culture. The "atomic hairdo," originally designed by GeeGee, hairstylist at the Flamingo, was a popular request for special occasions; the hair was pulled over a wire form shaped like a mushroom cloud and then sprinkled with silver glitter; the cost, $75.[72] The "atomic cocktail" was also a big seller in bars along the Strip; made from equal parts of vodka, brandy, and champagne with a dash of sherry, the potent drink was served at breakfast parties following the predawn shots.[73] Many of the hotels packed box lunches for bombwatchers to carry to picnics at Angel's Peak.[74] One establishment even called itself the Atomic View Motel because guests could witness the flash without ever leaving their lounge chairs.[75] In the Desert Inn Sky Room, pianist Ted Mossman first played his boogie woogie tune "Atomic Bomb Bounce," which soon had people dancing all over town.[76] Postcards were printed with the mushroom cloud rising in the background over "Glitter Gulch."

The Clark County official seal also displayed a large mushroom cloud, as did the 1953 yearbook cover for Las Vegas High School. The feature story for the June–December 1955 issue of *Nevada Highways and Parks* was about the NTS with a "typical, mushrooming cloud of fire, smoke, sand and radioactive particles" pictured on the cover.[77] Local merchants also played on the atomic theme; car salesman "Boob" Jones proudly advertised "Atom Drops on High Prices,"[78] and Allen and Hanson, Las Vegas haberdashers, placed a barrel full of broken plate glass window panes in front of their store with a sign, "Atomic Bomb Souvenirs—Free." Several casinos posted signs that warned if a tremor from a bomb blast caused the dice to turn or roulette balls to jump to another slot, the house man's ruling was final.[79] In Southern Nevada evidence of this atomic "mania" was widespread, and reflected the public's interest in the testing program, and belief in its necessity.

Epilogue

When atomic testing was moved underground late in 1963, the danger of fallout lessened as a matter of concern; many believed that radioactivity was now being contained far below the earth's surface where it could do no harm.[80] New issues drew the attention of the public and press away from the arms race; napalm, pickax handles, and love beads replaced the mushroom cloud as the star attraction on the 6 o'clock news. As the proliferation of nuclear weapons accelerated during the sixties and seventies, the public focus on atomic warfare and its dangers declined. Convinced of the necessity of first-strike power, and anesthetized by constant reassurances from the government that they could be safe in the event of nuclear attack, considerable segments of the American people had long since become accustomed to living with the bomb. As a result, the operations at the NTS slipped quietly into comparative obscurity.

Only one major local critic of the NTS arose during the late sixties: Howard Hughes, eccentric billionaire, big-time investor in Las Vegas, and ironically, the nation's largest prime defense contractor. Politically conservative, Hughes was not philosophically opposed to nuclear weapons; he only objected to their being tested near him or his hotels. He began a low-key campaign against the AEC in 1967, which escalated to a virtual war by the spring of 1968. Hughes contributed campaign funds to presidential candidates, lobbied the AEC, threatened to withdraw his investments from Las Vegas, and offered to pay any expenses which would result from delaying tests; he even wrote personally to President Johnson urging him to stop the testing program.[81] Interestingly, although Hughes had had little difficulty lining up press support for most of his Nevada resort projects, he was unable to convince the local papers to side with him against the AEC.[82] Shortly thereafter, Hughes' mental and physical health further deteriorated, and his interests turned elsewhere.

The NTS made the news again in a big way on December 18, 1970, when the "Baneberry" underground shot vented and sent a cloud of radioactive particles into the air.[83] The wind carried the cloud over area 12 where some 600 NTS employees were working and had to be evacuated. Three hundred of the workers were found to be contaminated and 20 were sent to the AEC laboratory for further observation and testing. Nominal precautions, such as showering, changing clothes, and washing their vehicles, were taken, but no one was found to need medical treatment.[84] The AEC reported that "the radiation presented no danger to human health or life and only the most minute traces of fallout were deposited on the ground."[85] Area 12 remained closed until after the New Year's holiday, but throughout the rest of the test site it was back to business as usual. No Nevada newspaper editorials or "letters to the editor" appeared criticizing the NTS and no official action was taken to interfere with its operations.

In the late seventies the issue of atmospheric testing hazards was revived. Medical findings indicated a higher than normal rate of leukemia among veterans who had participated in maneuvers at Camp Desert Rock and among residents who had lived "downwind" from the test site during the fifties.[86] Several Congressional hearings were convened;[87] President Carter named a task force to investigate the long-term effects of low level radiation;[88] and the Pentagon initiated a follow-up study of "atomic veterans."[89] Interest groups, including the Nevada Test Site Radiation Victims Association, the National Association of Atomic Veterans, Citizens Call, and the Committee of Survivors, were formed and began pressuring the federal government to admit negligence and compensate the alleged victims of atomic testing. Several court cases were also filed,[90] and legislation was introduced which would provide benefits to help pay medical expenses of those harmed by radioactive fallout.[91]

The reaction to these events in Nevada has been less than enthusiastic. The local papers covered the proceedings of the Salt Lake City case filed by "downwind residents" and the Baneberry case filed by two test site workers exposed during the 1970 venting, but there had been no public outcry about the validity of these claims. Although Nevada's representatives in Congress were cosponsors of the legislation to compensate "atomic victims," no mention was made of the bills by any of the parties during Nevada's heated political campaigns in 1982. Relatedly, no nuclear freeze question appeared on the ballot in Clark County, although it was a major issue in many areas.[92] And on January 27, 1983, the thirty-second anniversary of the first atmospheric shot at the NTS, a protest in front of the Federal Building drew only thirty marchers.[93] Though no official polls have been conducted, one is led to believe that, despite increasing evidence that activities at the NTS have caused damages in the past, the majority of southern Nevadans still support the test site and favor its continued operation in the state.[94]

Notes

1 Edgerton, Germeshausen and Green, Inc., "The Nevada Test Site and Southern Nevada," Report No. L-512 (March 15, 1961) p. 12, Special Collections, University of Nevada, Las Vegas, Library.

2 For detailed accounts of the development of the atomic bomb, see: Barton Bernstein. *The Atomic Bomb: The Critical Issues* (Boston: Little, Brown and Company, 1976); Anthony C. Brown and Charles B. MacDonald, editors, *The Secret History of the Atomic Bomb* (New York: Dial Press, 1979); Arthur H. Compton, *Atomic Quest* (New York: Oxford University Press, 1956); Leslie R. Groves, *Now It Can Be Told* (New York: Harper and Row, 1962); Lansing Lamont, *Day of Trinity* (New York: Atheneum, 1965); and Henry D. Smyth, *Atomic Energy for Military Purposes* (Princeton: Princeton University Press, 1945).

3 Lamont, p. 255.

4 Jonathon M. Weisgall, "The Nuclear Nomads of Bikini," *Foreign Policy* 39 (Summer 1980) p. 76.

5 Ibid.

6 The Marshall Islands were seized from Japan during World War II by the United States. They were placed under military control until July 1947, when the area became a U.N. strategic trust territory administered by the United States. See Robert C. Kiste, *The Bikinians* (Menlo Park, California: Cummings Publishers, 1974).

7 Ibid., pp. 86–90.

8 A 1967 AEC study found the area once again safe for human habitation and the Bikinians were returned to their homeland. It was a temporary arrangement, however. When subsequent radiological surveys indicated that Bikini was not safe, Secretary of Interior Rogers Morton interrupted the reconstruction and relocation process. He wrote to Secretary of Defense James Schlesinger in March 1975 requesting that a thorough survey of the area be undertaken. The Defense Department declined to take action because of the high costs of the proposed study. The Bikinians, frustrated and confused by the contradictory information they were receiving, filed suit in federal court in October 1975 to force the government to stop the resettlement program until such a survey was taken. The U.S. readily agreed to do so; but it was not until early 1978, after much internal bureaucratic squabbling, that the study was conducted. By March of that year, the atoll had been declared off limits and the inhabitants once again moved to nearby islands. The most recent reports indicate that the atoll may remain uninhabitable for at least another hundred years.

9 David Bradley, *No Place to Hide* (Boston: Little, Brown and Company, 1948); Stephen Hilgartner, Richard C. Bell, and Rory O'Connor, *Nukespeak* (New York: Penguin Books, 1983) pp. 72–74; William A. Shurcliff, *Bombs at Bikini: The Official Report of Operation Crossroads* (New York: William G. Wise, 1947) and Michael Uhl and Tod Ensign, *G.I. Guinea Pigs* (New York: Wideview Books 1980) pp. 30–43.

10 Howard L. Rosenberg, *Atomic Soldiers* (Boston: Beacon Press, 1980) p. 131.

11 Ibid.

12 Atomic Energy Commission, press release, December 1, 1947; National Association of Atomic Veterans, "Story of the Eniwetok Cleanup," *NAAV Newsletter* (November/December 1979) p. 14; Giff Johnson, "Paradise Lost," *Bulletin of the Atomic Scientists* 34 (December 1980) pp. 24–29; Uhl and Ensign, pp. 46–53.

13 The Soviets actually exploded their first atomic bomb on August 29, 1949, in Siberia. Although U.S. planes detected the fallout almost immediately, President Truman did not publicly announce the detonation until September 23, 1949. See: Herbert York, *The Advisors: Oppenheimer, Teller, and the Superbomb* (San Francisco: W. N. Freeman, 1976) pp. 33–35.

14 The Atomic Energy Commission was created by Congress with the passage of the Atomic Energy Act of 1946 (P.L. 585, 79th Congress, 60 stat 755). This act created a five member civilian commission, appointed by the President with the Senate's approval, which held a monopoly over nuclear technology at all levels. The Atomic Energy Commission was charged with certain objectives in the original legislation: . . . "subject at all times to the paramount objective of assuring the common defense and security, the development and utilization of atomic energy shall, so far as practical, be directed toward improving the public welfare, increasing the standard of living, strengthening free competition in private enterprise, and promoting world peace." See: Richard G. Hewlett and Oscar E. Anderson, *The New World, 1939–46: A History of the United States Atomic Energy Commission* (University Park, Pennsylvania: Penn State University Press, 1962.)

15 Aaron Smith, "Nuclear Weapons Testing in Nevada: History and Possible Health Effects," *Nevada Public Affairs Review* 1 (1982) pp. 5–11.

16 Rosenberg, pp. 25–31.

17 Los Alamos Scientific Laboratory, University of California, "Operation Ranger: Operational Program Reports," Vol. V (January–February, 1951).

18 Rosenberg, pp. 32–35.

19 Ibid., p. 37.

20 See: Ibid.; Uhl and Ensign, pp. 58–108; Thomas H. Saffer and Orville E. Kelly, *Countdown Zero* (New York: G. P. Putnam's Sons, 1982); George Washington University, Human Resources Research Office (HumRRO), "Desert Rock I, A Psychological Study of Troop Reaction to an Atomic Explosion," Technical Report No. 1 (February 1951); HumRRO, "Desert Rock IV: Reactions of an Armored Infantry Battalion to an Atomic Bomb Maneuver," Technical Report No. 2 (August 1953); HumRRO, "Desert Rock V: Reactions of Troop Participants and Forward Volunteer Officer Groups to Atomic Exercises," Information Report (August 1953); Johns Hopkins University Operations Research Office, "Troop Performance on a Training Maneuver Involving the Use of Atomic Weapons," (March 15 1952); and United States Army, *Exercise Desert Rock Information and Guide* (1951), available from the Fallout Records Centralization Project, Las Vegas, Nevada.

21 United States Department of Energy, "DOE's Nevada Operations Office: What It Does and Why" (July 1983) p. 1, United States Department of Energy, Las Vegas.

22 Ibid.; and United States Atomic Energy Commission, "Nevada Test Site" in *Nevada, The Silver State* (Carson City: Western States Historical Publishers, 1970) pp. 719–722, and United States Department of Energy, "Announced United States Nuclear Tests, July 1945–December 1982" (January 1983).

23 James H. McBride, *The Test Ban Treaty: Military, Technological and Political Implications* (Chicago: Henry Regnery Company, 1967).

24 Harry S. Truman, *Years of Trial and Hope* (Garden City: Doubleday and Company, 1955) Volume II of *Memoirs*, pp. 312–315.

25 In 1948 communists staged a coup in Czechoslovakia which replaced the existing government with one subservient to Moscow; that same year the Russians attempted to force Western Allies out of Berlin by blockading all land transportation routes into the city. In early 1949 forces led by Mao Tse-tung captured Peking and soon after established the People's Republic of China. And in June 1950 armed conflict broke out between North and South Korea which involved American participation against communist forces.

26 President Truman initiated an employee loyalty program in 1947; the practice was later intensified when President Eisenhower signed an executive order in April 1953 launching an unprecedented, far-reaching investigation into the loyalty of federal employees.

27 William F. Buckley, *The Committee and its Critics* (New York: Putnam, 1962); Robert K. Carr, *The House Committee on Un-American Activities, 1945–1950* (Ithaca: Cornell University Press, 1952); Athan G. Theokaris, *Seeds of Repression: Harry S. Truman and the Origins of McCarthyism* (Chicago: Quadrangle Books, 1971); Dalton Trumbo, *The Time of the Toad: A Study of Inquisition in America* (New York: Harper and Row, 1972).

28 Solomon A. Fineberg, *The Rosenberg Case* (New York: Oceana Publications, 1953); Louis Nizer, *The Implosion Conspiracy* (Garden City: Doubleday, 1973); and Jonathon Root, *The Betrayers; the Rosenberg Case—a Reappraisal of an American Crisis* (New York: Coward-McCann, 1963).

29 Regularly-scheduled air raid drills were held and public meetings were called to teach self-defense against nuclear attack through such measures as assuming correct physical positions during impact and washing off the radioactive fallout afterward. Dozens of how-to films were distributed; their names alone tell the story: "Pattern for Survival" (1950), "You Can Beat the A-Bomb" (1950), "Duck and Cover" (1951), and "Survival Under Atomic Attack " (1951).

30 Rosenberg; Uhl and Ensign; and Saffer and Kelly.

31 Typical of these was a widely-distributed, January 1951 Atomic Energy Commission statement which claimed that "Health and safety authorities have determined that no danger from or as a result of AEC activities may be expected. . . . All necessary precautions will be undertaken to insure that safety conditions are maintained." Similarly, in testimony before Congress in the spring of 1953, an AEC official reported that fallout from atmospheric testing was no more dangerous than medical x-rays. In a *U.S. News and World Report* article (March 25, 1955, pp. 21–26) AEC Commissioner Willard Libby cited evidence from AEC research which indicated that bomb fallout "would not likely be at all dangerous." And Edward Teller, arguing for continued testing in *Life Magazine* (February 10, 1958, pp. 64–66) claimed that radiation from fallout "might be slightly beneficial or have no effect at all."

32 United States Atomic Energy Commission, "Atomic Test Effects in the Nevada Test Site Region" (January 1955), Nevada Historical Society, Las Vegas.

33 Ibid., p. 23.

34 The Iron County sheepherders carried their case to the Supreme Court in 1955 (*Bullock v. U.S.* 145 F. Supp. 827) but their claims were denied based on expert testimony presented by the government which "proved" that radiation had not caused the animal deaths and deformities. The case was recently ordered reopened on August 4, 1982, however, by Judge Sherman Christenson on grounds that the government had been "intentionally false and deceptive. "

35 Nineteen of the twenty-one children of the island of Rongelap who were under twelve at the time of exposure subsequently developed thyroid tumors, forcing the government to pass the Bikini Compensation Act of 1964, which appropriated $950,000 to be distributed among the victims. This act was amended on October 15, 1977, when Congress passed P.L. 95–134 to include the inhabitants of nearby Uterik, who were also exposed to the "Bravo" cloud and suffered radiation-related illnesses.

36 Ralph E. Lapp, *The Voyage of the Lucky Dragon* (New York: Harper and Brothers Publishers, 1957); and Stephen Salaff, "The Lucky Dragon," *Bulletin of the Atomic Scientists* 34 (May 1978) pp. 21–23.

37 *New York Times* (April 1, 1954) p. 20.

38 Only two months after dropping the bombs on Japan, President Truman told a joint session of Congress that "the hope of civilization lies in . . . renunciation of the use and development of the atomic bomb." He urged all nations to join the United States in developing atomic energy solely for peaceful purposes. Uhl and Ensign, p. 32.

39 Atomic Energy Commission press release, December 22, 1947, National Archives, Washington, D.C.

40 Edwin B. Eckel, *Nevada Test Site*, Geological Society of America, Inc., Memoir 110 (1968) p. 2.

41 Albin J. Dahl, *Nevada's Southern Economy*, Research Report No. 8 (Carson City: University of Nevada, College of Business Administration. March 1969), pp. 23–30.

42 A. Costandina Titus, "Back to Ground Zero: Old Footage Through New Lenses," *Journal of Popular Film and Television* 11 (Spring 1983) pp. 2–11.

43 By 1970 about 15,000 scouts had qualified for this merit badge, according to the *Annual Report of Congress of the Atomic Energy Commission for 1969* (January 1970) p. 211.

44 Hilgartner, Bell, and O'Connor, pp. 74–78.

45 For example, in 1953 when Robert Oppenheimer, former director of the Manhattan Project, publicly opposed the development of the H-bomb, he was charged with maintaining communist associations and acting in a way designed to promote the best interests of the Russians, his security clearance was cancelled and his long-term government service was ended. See: Phillip M. Stern, *The Oppenheimer Case: Security on Trial* (New York: Harper and Row, 1969); and York. And in 1957 when Linus Pauling, Nobel prizewinner in chemistry, led a petition drive by scientists in opposition to atmospheric testing, President Eisenhower, in a press conference, implied that the petition was the work of an "organization" which did not have the best interests of the nation in mind. Pauling was also called before the House Un-American Activities Committee which further investigated his anti-nuclear connections. See: Linus Pauling, *No More War* (New York: Dodd, Mead, 1958) pp. 160–172.

46 Harvey Wasserman and Norman Solomon, *Killing Our Own* (New York: Dell Publishing Company, 1982) pp. 92–101.

47 The final vote was 56,049 for Eisenhower and 40,640 for Stevenson. *Political History of Nevada, 1979* (Carson City: State Printing Office), p. 226.

48 Douglas T. Miller and Marion Nowak, *The Fifties: The Way We Really Were* (New York: Doubleday, 1977) p. 413.

49 Ibid., p. 63.

50 Ibid., p. 80. In 1958 four pacifists in a thirty-foot ketch, the *Golden Rule,* tried to sail from Hawaii to Eniwetok; they were detained and arrested by the United States Coast Guard.

51 There were a few instances during the early days of atmospheric testing in which certain individuals expressed opposition to the program. Windows were shattered and some horses were burned by radioactive fallout. However, the Atomic Energy Commission was quick to reimburse local citizens for these property losses, and thus keep complaints to a minimum. One especially dissatisfied resident was Dan Sheahan, owner of the Groom Mine located some thirty-eight miles north of the Nevada Test Site; Sheahan complained that he had to shut down operations during test blasts and this was a great inconvenience and expense for his business. Such protests were the exception, however, not the rule.

52 In response to the needs of the new NTS, some 3000 jobs were created between 1951 and 1958, when the voluntary moratorium went into effect; by 1968, this labor force had increased to 10,187, representing a gross annual payroll of $122.2 million. During the same decade and a half, government investments in the program totaled over $178.8 million. In 1980 the physical plant was valued in excess of $300 million and the operating budget for that year alone was $345 million. See: Dahl, pp. 36–38; Russell R. Elliott, *History of Nevada* (Lincoln, University of Nebraska Press, 1973) pp. 339–341; Joseph A. Fry, "The History of Defense Spending in Nevada: Preview of the MX," in Francis X. Hartigan, editor, *MX in Nevada: A Humanistic Perspective* (Reno: Nevada Humanities Committee, 1980) pp. 37–43; and Mary Ellen Glass, *Nevada's Turbulent Fifties* (Reno: University of Nevada Press, 1981) pp. 43–46

53 Jerome E. Edwards, *Pat McCarran: Political Boss of Nevada* (Reno: University of Nevada Press, 1982).

54 Rosenberg, p. 32.

55 Sister Margaret P. McCarran, "Patrick Anthony McCarran: 1876–1954," Part II, *Nevada Historical Society Quarterly* 12 (Spring 1969) p. 50; *Las Vegas Review Journal* (May 26, 1953) p. 1.

56 Danial Lang, "Our Far Flung Correspondents: Blackjack and Flashes," *New Yorker* 8 (September 20, 1952) p. 97.

63 *Las Vegas Sun* (March 13, 1955) p. 1.

64 *Las Vegas Review-Journal* (March 11, 1955) p.1.

65 Ibid. (March 22, 1955) p. 1.

66 Ibid. (January 15, 1951) p. 1.

67 *Las Vegas Sun* (January 30, 1951) p. 1.

68 *Las Vegas Review-Journal* (May 24, 1953) p. 4.

69 Uhl and Ensign pp. 76–77, 82–83.

70 "Operation 'Doom Town'," *Nevada Highways and Parks* 13 (June–December 1952) pp. 1–17.

71 *Las Vegas Review-Journal* (May 6, 1955) p. 1.

72 Ibid. (October 18, 1955) p. 4.

73 Lang, p. 91.

74 Georgia Lewis, "'Atomized' Las Vegas Danced 'Atomic Boogie'," *Las Vegas Review-Journal*, "The Nevadan" (January 23, 1983) pp. 6L–7L, 13L.

75 Uhl and Ensign, p. 77.

76 Lang, pp. 95–96.

77 "Operation 'Doom Town'," p. 1.

78 Rosenberg, p. 82.

79 Lang, p. 90.

80 While the problem of radioactivity seemed to be solved, some feared that underground testing could cause earthquakes. Dr. Alan Ryall, a University of Nevada geologist, stated that "effects due to the continued firing of large underground tests would be cumulative, possibly eventually resulting in a sizable earthquake." See Elliott, p. 339.

81 Donald L. Barlett and James B. Steele, *Empire: The Life, Legend, and Madness of Howard Hughes* (New York: W. W. Norton and Company, 1979) pp. 340–347.

82 Ibid., p. 341.

83 Paul Duckworth, *Baneberry: A Nuclear Disaste*r (Las Vegas: Harris Printers, Inc., 1976).

86 Ibid.; *Las Vegas Review-Journal* (December 19–21, 1970) p. 1; and *Las Vegas Sun* (December 19–21, 1970) p. 1.

85 *Las Vegas Review-Journal* (December 20, 1970) p. 1.

86 "Smoky and Leukemia: High Rate Confirmed," *Science News* (October 3, 1980) p. 118; Glyn G. Caldwell, et al., "Leukemia Among Participants in Military Maneuvers at a Nuclear Bomb Test," *Journal of American Medical Association* 244 (October 1980) pp. 1575–1578; Joseph L. Lyon, et al., "Childhood Leukemias Associated With Fallout from Nuclear Testing," *New England Journal of Medicine* 300 (February 1979) pp. 39–402; and Edward S. Weiss, et al., "Thyroid Modularity in Southwestern Utah School Children Exposed to Fallout Radiation," *American Journal of Public Health* 61 (1971).

87 U.S. Congress, House Committee on Health and the Environment, Hearings, 95th Congress, 2nd Session (January 1978); U.S. Congress, Senate Committee on Veterans' Affairs, Hearings, 96th Congress, 1st Session (June 1979); U.S. Congress, House Committee on Interstate and Foreign Commerce, Subcommittee on Oversight and Investigations, Hearings, 96th Congress, 2nd Session (August 1980).

88 The Interagency Task Force on the Health Effects of Ionizing Radiation was headed by Peter Libassi; its report, issued to the public in July 1979, concluded that radiation may cause irreparable change in cells, resulting in cancer, developmental abnormalities, and genetic damage.

89 Efforts were made to identify all the soldiers who had participated in atomic test maneuvers, and toll free telephone lines were installed so that "atomic veterans" could check in from anywhere in the country to get information on their dosage levels, etc. See: Saffer and Kelly, pp. 177–179; and Uhl and Ensign, p. 91.

90 A class action suit was filed in Salt Lake City on August 30, 1979, by 1200 "downwind residents" charging the government with negligence: *Allen v. U.S.* (CA No. C-79–515). The widows of two test site workers filed suit following the Baneberry incident: *Dorothy Roberts v. U.S.* (Civil LV. 1766 RDF) and *Louise Nunamaker v. U.S.* (Civil LV. 76–259 RDF). Several cases have also been filed by "atomic veterans": *Jaffee v. U.S.* (79–1543, February 20, 1980) and *Broudy v. U.S.* (79–3829, June 18, 180). To date, not one of these cases has been decided in favor of the plaintiff.

91 Recent radiation compensation bills include H.R. 4766 introduced by Representative Gunn McKay on July 12, 1979; S. 1865 by Senator Edward Kennedy on October 4, 1979; H.R. 872 by Representative Henry Gonzales on January 16, 1981; H.R. 1564 by Representative Norman Mineta on February 5, 1981; H.R. 2229 by Representative Tony Coelho on March 2, 1981; H.R. 4012 by Representative Robert Davis on June 25, 1981; S. 1483 by Senator Orrin Hatch on July 14, 1981; and H.R. 6052 by Representative Dan Marriott on April 1, 1982. These bills all died in committee. Currently pending in the Senate is S. 921 introduced on March 21, 1983, by Senator Hatch (R) of Utah this bill calls for pro-rated payments of awards up to $500,000 to people who suffer from radiation- related illness as a result of exposure to fallout from atmospheric testing. See A. Costandina Titus, "Governmental Responsibility for Victims of Atomic Testing: A Chronicle of the Politics of Compensation," *Journal of Health Politics, Policy and Law* 8 (Summer 1983) pp. 277–292.

92 The Clark County Commissioners kept the question off the ballot with a vote of 4 against, 1 in favor.

93 *Las Vegas Review Journal* (January 28, 1983) p. 1B.

94 The author wishes to thank Ms. Vera Thompson, Mr. David Millman, and the class of POS 408b (Summer Session II, 1983) for their research assistance.

from *Earthtones*
(1995)

Ann Ronald

Professor Ann Ronald of the Department of English at the University of Nevada, Reno, has written extensively on the West, its literature and its environment. Ronald is quick to challenge those who view Nevada's landscape as barren and unappealing. The following essay, excerpted from her 1995 collaborative work with photographer Stephen Trimble, introduces the reader to a Nevada most people have seldom observed, a land of subtle colors and hues, of hidden sanctuaries of wild animals and birds, of starkly beautiful mountain peaks and wondrously intriguing canyons located far off the paved highway. "Since moving to Nevada," she writes, "I've adopted an aesthetic that embraces horizons unencumbered by the niceties most tourists enjoy, that unabashedly appreciates this special earthtone landscape. Accustomed now to remoteness and rattlers, I've taught myself to get over the color green. Along the way I've fallen in love, I confess, with Nevada's well-wrought terrain."

Too many people picture Nevada landscape the way eastern newspaper reporters and urban advertising agencies imagine it. High-Rise Casinos and High-Tech Theme Parks. Frank Sinatra and Barbra Streisand. Liberal Slots, Computerized Poker, Craps. A Get-Rich-Quick Mentality. Glamour, High Rollers, Spectacle. Holiday neon punctuating empty terrain. The previous generation's Nuclear Test Site. The next century's Hazardous Waste Dump. Mile after mile after mile of America's Loneliest Roads.

Few tourists, few essayists, few photographers bother with the sparse horizons beyond the neon, the lonely wilderness spaces of California's less comely neighbor to the east. Writing five short essays now collected in *Steep Trails* John Muir set what I consider an unfortunate aesthetic tone. He described Nevada scenery as "a singularly barren aspect, appearing gray and forbidding and shadeless." Even though Muir admired some isolated peaks and valleys, he generally treated the Nevada landscape harshly. Calling the Silver State "this thirsty land," he imagined it "like heaps of ashes dumped from the blazing sky" and summarized his feelings by envisioning "one vast desert, all sage and sand, hopelessly irredeemable now and forever."

Someone blankly staring through a car window might well agree with Muir's dry assessment. Rivers are few and far between. Interstate 80 stretches across a lot of sand and sage, with only an occasional glimpse of the evaporating Humboldt that weary pioneers trailed 150 years ago. Highways 50 and 93 and 95 alternate sinewy mountain passes with flats of alkali and dust, relieved only by winter snow or summer cloudbursts. None of these major routes is scenic in any conventional way.

Nor are the views from an airplane window any more obviously picturesque. While a casual traveler might glance once or twice at the striations of brown, chocolate, and beige, might briefly puzzle over the shadowed ridgelines, might even shake his or her head at the vacant horizons below, most find more pleasure in the refreshments being served. My seatmate last October, making idle conversation, echoed the Illinois couple overheard at an interstate rest stop two months before: 'What is there to see out there?" "It's so empty." "It's so drab." "It's so depressing."

One of Wallace Stegner's essays, "Thoughts in a Dry Land," touches briefly on why we are unable to change our aesthetic minds about what is scenic and what is not. He insists that we have to get over the color green. Stegner is right, of course. Almost all of us have been taught a worldview that prefers green and blue to ocher and beige, that values redwoods and oceans more than rabbitbrush and sinks. Stegner concludes by saying that we inherently lack appreciation for such things as sagebrush and raw earth and alkali flats. These, he suggests, are acquired tastes, ones not easily adopted by conventional sensibilities.

Empty space, and the concomitant exposure of geologic time, are acquired tastes too. As someone who grew up in the forested Pacific Northwest, I not only was indoctrinated by the beauty of green but I also was comforted by vine maple, maidenhair ferns, and shin tangle. The near view—perhaps a high meadow filled with purple gentian, perhaps the riffle of a stream—was pleasingly, narrowly defined. Any long view was supposed to be grandiose in a European kind of way, punctuated by two-hundred-foot Douglas fir and glaciated peaks with romantic-sounding names. I possessed no imaginative comprehension for the shapes and shades of basin and rockbound range in a "'land of little rain."

Now that I've spent nearly twenty-five years tracking such desert distances, however, I've developed a very different aesthetic eye. From the air, I ignore my seatmate's imprecations and look down on a Jackson Pollock oil. Framed by the plane's window, the colors stipple from black-topped ridges to creamy basins with pale cuts muted red, like dried blood. Curved washes narrow, then widen, then narrow again. The trace of a river twists into tight coils, a series of oxbows unwilling to dry themselves out. The shadows that follow the oxbows are metallic tints from a desiccated palette. Sere green—not emerald hues, but tones befitting the jaded contours of the land below.

Closer to the ground, heading east to west across a lonely highway, I picture not a gallery hung with postmodern paintings but a film unrolling before my eyes. Rounded hills fold into wrinkled cavities, amber curves sharpen against a darker sky. An evening raincloud spills from its top a Niagara that will never reach the earth. Three mustangs browse silently through the yellowed grasses. At the sound of my truck approaching, two golden eagles erupt from the pavement. One, clutching a roadkill rabbit, flies off; the other, settling on a nearby fencepost, glares at the highway. I stop the truck, grab my binoculars, and stare back at the huge bird.

That's what the man and woman from Illinois might have seen, had they known that scenery need not be green, that shapes and shadows may segue into figures and forms, and that seductive details can be spotted when one goes slow. If they had strolled out into the sage, they might have discovered how much a single lens can reveal. In springtime the brown hills turn lime velvet for a week or maybe a month. Even after a dry winter, showy phlox the size of my little fingernail cluster underfoot and alongside abandoned dirt roads, while a wet winter brings forth a patchwork of purple lupine. Blizzard white transforms lumpish limestone blocks into peaks reminiscent of the Alps, while cloud shadows in any season writhe the distance into a close-up kaleidoscope of colored motion.

Too many visitors to the Silver State never see my Great Basin. Or, if they do see it, they don't know how to describe it. Their Nevada is a preconceived one, a product of instinct, intuition, and intellects unwilling to look favorably at dry desert scenery. Their Nevada, I'm afraid, is an unfortunate cliché. *Earthtones: A Nevada Album* presumes to refute this point of view. Neither "a singularly barren aspect" nor a landscape "hopelessly irredeemable, now and forever," our Nevada is one seen through sympathetic eyes.

Teal sky and a sea of purple sage. Mountain mahogany, white fir, a crimson mass of claret cup cactus. Rawhide Springs and Green Monster Canyon. A bobcat tiptoeing along Corn Creek. Desert tortoise, a marmot whistling for his mate, a nesting long-eared owl. The Black Rock playa, Lake Lahontan. Currant Mountain and Duckwater Peak, Rainbow Canyon and Calico Hills. Limestone, sandstone, and tuff. One stone wall, a few broken bricks; dry alfalfa, an empty irrigation ditch. A dust-blown sunset, vermilion and orange and gold. "One vast desert?" Not exactly. One vast deserted landscape of color and shadow and aesthetic dimension.

"Las Vegas, U.S.A."
(1994)

Kurt Andersen

Tom Wolfe's exotic essay on Las Vegas in the mid-1960s drew attention to new trends that were unique to the "twenty-four hour" entertainment center of Las Vegas. By 1994, those trends had, according to Time *magazine feature writer Kurt Andersen, become a new standard for American popular culture. His far-ranging cover story identified Las Vegas as the crucible for post-modernist America. Long the butt of jokes and the subject of searing moralistic criticism, Andersen notes Las Vegas no longer stood out from the rest of post-modern American society—which had embraced many of Nevada's once-condemned social and cultural norms, be they popular music, 24-hour businesses, sexually explicit entertainment, gambling, or easy divorce. Much of American popular culture, Andersen concludes, has become "pervasively Vegasy."*

How can a large-spirited American not like Las Vegas, or at least smile at the notion of it? On the other hand, how can any civilized person not loathe Las Vegas, or at least recoil at its relentlessness?

How can you not love and hate a city so crazily go-go that three different, colossally theme-park-like casino-hotels (the $375 million Luxor, Steve Wynn's $475 million Treasure Island and now the $1 billion MGM Grand, the largest hotel on earth and the venue last weekend for Barbra Streisand's multimillion-dollar return to live, paid performing) have opened on the Strip in just the past three months? How can you not love and hate a city so freakishly democratic that at a hotel called the Mirage, futuristic-looking infomercial star Susan Powter and a premodern Mennonite family can pass in a corridor, neither taking note of the other? How can you not love and hate a city where the $100,000 paintings for sale at an art gallery appended to Caesars Palace (Patron: "He's a genius." Gallery employee: "Yes, he's so creative." Patron: "It gives me goose bumps") are the work of Anthony Quinn?

In no other peacetime locale are the metaphors and ironies so impossibly juicy, so ripe for the plucking. And there are always new crops of redolent, suggestive Vegas facts, of which any several—for instance: the Mirage has a $500-a-pull slot-machine salon; the lung-cancer death rate here is the second highest in the country; the suicide rate and cellular-phone usage are the highest—constitute a vivid, up-to-date sketch of the place.

But it used to be that while Las Vegas was unfailingly piquant and over the top, it was *sui generis*, its own highly peculiar self. Vegas in none of its various phases (ersatz Old West outpost in the 1930s and '40s, gangsters-meet-Hollywood high-life oasis in the '50s and '60s, uncool polyester dump in the '70s and early '80s) was really an accurate prism through which to regard the nation as a whole.

Now, however, as the city ricochets through its biggest boom since the Frank-and-Dino Rat Pack days of the '50s and '60s the tourist inflow has nearly doubled over the past decade, and the area remains among America's fastest growing—the hypereclectic 24-hour-a-day fantasy-themed party machine no longer seems so very exotic or extreme. High-tech spectacle, convenience, classlessness, loose money, a Nikes-and-T-shirt dress code: that's why immigrants flock to the U.S.; that's why some 20 million Americans (and 2 million foreigners) went to Vegas in 1992. "Las Vegas exists because it is a perfect reflection of America," says Steve Wynn, the city's most important and interesting resident. "You say 'Las Vegas' in Osaka or Johannesburg, anywhere in the world, and people smile, they understand. It represents all the things people in every city in America like. Here they can get it in one gulp." There is a Jorge Luis Borges story called The Aleph that describes the magical point where all places are seen from every angle. Las Vegas has become that place in America, less because of its own transformation in the past decade than because of the transformation of the nation. Las Vegas has become Americanized, and, even more, America has become Las Vegasized.

With its ecologically pious displays of white tigers and dolphins—and no topless show girls—the almost tasteful Mirage has profoundly enlarged and updated the notion of Vegas amusement since it opened in 1989. The general Las Vegas marketing spin today is that the city is fun for the whole family. It seems to be an effective public relations line, but it's an idea that the owners of the new Luxor and MGM Grand may have taken too much to heart.

Inside the Luxor is a fake river and barges, plus several huge "participatory adventure" areas, an ersatz archaeological ride, as well as a two-story Sega virtual-reality video-game arcade. The joint has acres of casino space—but the slots and blackjack tables are, astoundingly, quite separate from and mostly concealed by the Disneyesque fun and games. The bells and whistles are more prominent and accessible than the casino itself, and are not merely a cute, quick way to divert people as they proceed into the fleecing pen. The MGM Grand has gone further: it spent hundreds of millions of dollars extra to build an adjacent but entirely separate amusement park, cramming seven rides (three involving fake rivers) and eight "themed areas" onto 33 acres, less than a 10th the size of Disney World.

The smart operators, such as Wynn, understand the proper Vegas meaning of family fun: people who won't take vacations without their children now have places to stick the kids while Mom and Dad pursue the essentially unwholesome act of squandering the family savings on cards and dice. "It's one thing for the place to be user-friendly to the whole family because the family travels together," Wynn says. "It's quite a different thing to sit down and dedicate creative design energy to build for children. I'm not, ain't gonna, not interested. I'm after Mom and Dad." Wynn's dolphins are just a '90s form of free Scotch and sodas, a cheap, subtler means of inducing people to leave their room and lose money.

But even if Vegas is not squeaky clean, even if its raison d'etre remains something other than provoking a childlike sense of wonder, the place is no longer considered racy or naughty by most people. It seems incredible today that a book in the '60s about the city was called Las Vegas, City of Sin? The change in perception is mainly because Americans' collective tolerance for vulgarity has gone way, way up. Just a decade ago, "hell" and "damn" were the most offensive words permitted on broadcast TV; today the colloquialisms "butt" and "sucks" are in daily currency on all major networks. Characters on Fox sitcoms and MTV cartoon shows snicker about their erections, and the stars of NYPD Blue can call each other "asshole." Look at Montel Williams and Geraldo. Listen to Howard Stern.

In Vegas, Wynn actually gets a little defensive about his nudity-free shows ("Hey, I'm not afraid of boobies"), the streets are hookerless, and the best-known Vegas strip club, the Palomino, lies discretely beyond the city limits. Meanwhile, at 116 Hooters restaurants in 30 states, the whole point is the battalion of bosomy young waitresses in tight-fitting tank tops who exist as fantasy objects for a clientele of high-testosterone frat boys and young bubbas. No wonder middle Americans find the idea of bringing kids along to Vegas perfectly appropriate. How ironic that two decades after Hunter Thompson's book *Fear and Loathing in Las Vegas,* countercultural ripple effects have so raised the American prudishness threshold that Las Vegas is considered no more unseemly than any other big city.

Sixteen years ago, Nevada was the only place in America where one could legally go to a casino, and there were just fourteen state lotteries. As recently as 1990, there were just three states with casinos, not counting those on Indian reservations; now there are nine. Lotteries have spread to 37 states. Indiana and five Mississippi River states have talked themselves into allowing gambling on riverboats—hey, it's not immoral it's, you know, historical—and such floating casinos may soon be moored off Boston and in Philadelphia as well. Sensible, upright Minnesota, of all places, now has more casinos than Atlantic City. With only one state, Hawaii, retaining a ban on gambling, and with cable-TV oligarch John Malone interested in offering gambling on the information superhighway, Vegas doesn't seem sinful, just more entertaining and shameless.

And fortunate, especially in this age of taxophobia and budget freezes. The state of Nevada now derives half its public funds from gaming-related revenues—from voluntary consumption taxes, nearly all paid by out-of-staters. Nevadans pay no state income or inheritance tax. To craven political leaders elsewhere, this looks pretty irresistible: no pain, all gain, vigorish as fiscal policy. A new report from the Center for the Study of the States concluded, however, that "gambling cannot generally produce enough tax revenue to significantly reduce reliance on other taxes or to solve a serious state fiscal problem."

One of the defining features of Las Vegas has been its 24-hour commercial culture, which arose as a corollary to 24-hour casinos: Along with the University of Nevada's basketball team, it is the great source of civic pride. It is the salient urban feature first mentioned by Harvard-educated physician Mindy Shapiro about her adopted city: "You can buy a Cuisinart or drop off your dry cleaning at 4 in the morning!" The comic magician Penn Jillette, who was performing at Bally's last week, marvels, "There are no good restaurants, but at least they're open at 3 in the morning."

But Las Vegas' retail ceaselessness is no longer singular. These days around-the-clock restaurants and supermarkets are unremarkable in hyperconvenient America, and the information superhighway, even in its current embryonic state, permits people everywhere to consume saucy entertainment—whether pay-per-view pornography or dating by modem with strangers—at any time of the day or night.

Las Vegas was created as the world's first experiential duty-free zone, a place dedicated to the anti-Puritan pursuit of instant gratification—no waiting, no muss, no fuss. In the '30s, Nevada was famous for its uniquely quick and easy marriage (and divorce) laws. And although a certain kind of demented Barbie and Ken still make it a point to stage their weddings in Las Vegas (158,470 people married there in 1992, a majority of them out-of-staters), it is now an atavistic impulse, since the marriage and divorce laws in the rest of the U.S. have long since caught up with Nevada's pioneering looseness.

When instant gratification becomes a supreme virtue, pop culture follows. Siegfried and Roy, the un-Vegas magicians (imagine, if you dare, a hybrid of Liberace, Arnold Schwarzenegger, David Copperfield and Marlin Perkins) who perform 480 shows a year in their own theater at the Mirage, don't seem satisfied unless every trick is a show-stopper and every moment has the feel of a finale. In front of the new Treasure Island is a Caribbean-cum-Mediterranean faux village fronting a 65-ft.-deep "lagoon" in which a full-scale British man-of-war and pirate vessel every 90 minutes stage a battle with serious fires, major explosions, 22 actors, stirring music, a sinking ship. It is very impressive, completely satisfying—and gives spectators pretty much everything in 15 minutes, for free, that they go to certain two-hour, $65-a-seat Broadway musicals for.

In the '50s and '60s Vegas impresarios took a dying strain of vaudeville and turned it into a highly particular Vegas style. Gamblers from Duluth and Atlanta came to see only-in-Vegas entertainments: Sinatra, Streisand, stand-up comedians, the trash rococo of Liberace, both flaunting and denying his gayness; hot-ticket singer-dancers like Ann-Margret, and shows with whiffy themes that existed as mere pretexts for bringing out brigades of suggestively costumed young women jiggling through clouds of pastel-colored smoke as over-amped pop tunes blared. It was cheesy glamour, to be sure, but it was rare and one of a kind.

Precisely when did Vegas values start leaching deep into the American entertainment mainstream? Was it when Sammy Davis Jr. got his own prime-time variety show on NBC in 1966, or a year later, when both Jerry Lewis and Joey Bishop had network shows running? Or in the summer of 1969, when Elvis Presley staged his famous 14-show-a-week comeback gig in Vegas?

Whenever the change began, American show business is today so pervasively Vegasy that we hardly notice anymore. The arty, sexy French-Canadian circus Cirque du Soleil had its breakthrough run in Manhattan before decamping this year to Las Vegas, and neither venue seemed unnatural. Big rock-'n'-roll concerts nowadays are often as much about wowie-kazowie production values—giant video walls, neon, fireworks, suggestively costumed young men and women, clouds of pastel-colored smoke—as music. Michael Jackson's highly stylized shtick—the cosmetics, the wardrobe, the not-quite-dirty bumps and grinds, the Liberace-like gender-preference coyness—is so Vegas that the city embraced him at every turn: a Jackson impersonator is a star of the Riviera's long-running show Splash; Jackson plays a spaceship commander in one of Sega's new virtual-reality video games at the Luxor; and Siegfried and Roy got the real Jackson to compose and sing their show-closing theme song, Mind Is the Magic. And Madonna? Her just finished Girlie Show world tour, with its Vegas-style dancers and meretricious Vegas-style lighting, is precisely as pseudosexy in 1993 as shows at the Flamingo were in 1963—decadence lite.

Back when the Rat Pack ruled, Jackie Mason played Vegas and Edward Albee was on Broadway. Today essentially idea-free spectacle—The Phantom of the Opera, Cats—dominates New York City so-called legitimate theater, and stand-up comedy is ubiquitous. In the '90s, Friars Club comedians like Mason have hit Broadway shows, and Andrew Lloyd Webber's Broadway musical Starlight Express has been permanently installed in the showroom of the Las Vegas Hilton. The crossbreeding seems complete.

Penn and Teller are ultra-show-biz-savvy New York intellectuals whose act is an ironic deconstruction of magic shows in addition to being a very impressive magic show. They first played Vegas a year ago. Penn Jillette's fondness for Vegas, like every hip baby boomer's, is sweet-and-sour, simultaneously bemused and fond. Of a traditional Vegas variety show at Bally's called Jubilee, he rants, "In the first five minutes they destroy temples and sink a giant model of the Titanic—there are 80 topless dancing women while the Titanic sinks, blast furnaces spewing fire. You look around you, and every single person in the crowd perceives it ironically. Every single person in the show perceives it ironically. It seems like everybody in Vegas nowadays is too hip to be in Vegas."

Serious connoisseurs of the surrealistically kitschy visit Graceland Wedding Chapel, where Norm Jones, the Elvis impersonator in residence, is both pleased and bewildered by the sudden popularity of the wedding ceremonies he performs for $250. Heavy-metal star Jon Bon Jovi got married there in 1989; Phil Joanou, director of the U2's concert film Rattle and Hum, was not only married at the Graceland Chapel but played a tape of his wedding onstage every night of the band's last American tour. In December 1992 three members of Def Leppard showed up at the door, one to get married and two to renew their vows.

Last year 8 million of the city's 22 million visitors were under 40, and nearly half of those were under 30. When Soul Asylum, as part of the MTV-sponsored 1993 Alternative Nation tour, landed at its last U.S. stop in Las Vegas, the band deviated from its song list to belt out Vegasy tunes like Mandy and Rhinestone Cowboy. Luke Perry and Jason Priestley of Beverly Hills, 90210, huge Tom Jones fans, recently flew to Vegas to see their hero sing, and members of the Red Hot Chili Peppers went to Las Vegas to see and meet Julio Iglesias. "Suddenly the same things I was doing five years ago that were considered pure corn are now perceived to be in," says Wayne Newton. "It's a wonderful satisfaction to finally be hip."

Long before this generation of young hipsters started reveling in the Vegas gestalt, certain intellectuals were taking seriously the city's no-holds-barred urban style. It was 25 years ago that a little-known architect and professor, Robert Venturi, returned to Yale with his two dozen student acolytes after a remarkable 10-day expedition to Las Vegas, where they stayed at the Stardust. His influential 1972 book, *Learning From Las Vegas,* immediately made Venturi famous as a heretical high-culture proponent for the ad hoc, populist design of the Strip—the giant neon signs, the kitschy architectural allusions to ancient Rome and the Old West, any zany kind of skin-deep picturesqueness. And a decade later, the fringe tendency became a full-fledged movement: Post-Modernism.

Today almost every big-city downtown has new scrapers that endeavor to look like old skyscrapers. Almost every suburb has a shopping center decorated with phony arches, phony pediments, phony columns. Two decades after Venturi proposed, with the intellectual's standard perverse quasi-affection, that Vegas could be a beacon for the nation's architecture, his manifesto had transformed America. Forget the Bauhaus and your house—it is the Vegas aesthetic, architecture as grandiose cartoon, that has become the American Establishment style. And so the splendidly pyramidal new Luxor and cubist new MGM Grand (both the work of local architect Veldon Simpson) do not seem so weird, since equally odd buildings now exist all over the place.

As it was being created in the '50s, Vegas' Strip was a mutant kind of American main drag, an absurdly overscaled Main Street for cars instead of people. Everywhere else in the country the shopping mall was replacing the traditional downtown. But now the Strip in Las Vegas has come full circle, its vacant stretches filling in with so many new hotels and casinos that what had been the ultimate expression of car culture has masses of tourists walking from Bally's to Caesars to Treasure Island, and from the Luxor to the Excalibur to the MGM Grand. The Strip is virtually an old-fashioned Main Street.

Meanwhile malls, the fin-de-sicle scourge of genuine Main Streets, have become preposterous Vegasy extravaganzas themselves—themed, entertainment driven, all-inclusive, overwhelming. The West Edmonton Mall in Alberta, with its 119 acres of stores and restaurants and the world's largest indoor amusement park, pulled in 22 million people in 1992, as many as visited Las Vegas; and the 16-month-old Mall of America outside Minneapolis, with only 96 acres of money-spending opportunity and America's largest indoor amusement park, claimed 40 million visitors in its first year.

Yet even as the rest of America has become more and more like Las Vegas, life for Vegas residents as well as visitors is more thoroughly sugar-frosted with fantasy than any where else. "Our customers want a passive experience," says Wynn, "but romantic." Such as his ersatz South Seas restaurant, Kokomos ("Kokomos—this is better than Hawaii. There's no place in the South Pacific where the light is so perfect, so beautiful"). At the Mediterranean-themed resort Wynn envisions for the new Dunes site down the Strip, he has talked of creating a kind of raffish virtual Nazism: at a casino-restaurant modeled on Rick's casino-restaurant in Casablanca, scenes from the movie would seamlessly blend with live actors playing Bogart and the movie's other characters among the paying customers.

The new Las Vegas has even fabricated a bit of ersatz old Las Vegas: along with its Oriental- and Bahamian-themed suites, the MGM offers rooms themed according to a decorator's Vegas ideal. The Sands, one of the last intact artifacts of the Rat Pack golden era, is being remodeled to within an inch of its life. "We're going to theme, definitely," the hotel's public relations spokeswoman said as work was beginning late last year. "But we don't know what the themes are yet."

Even civilians must theme. At the Lakes, an upscale housing complex, the developer has built a whole tract of Gothic minicastles, one next to the other. Mountain Spa, a high-end resort and corporate retreat now being plotted on 640 acres in the city's northwest, will have a "Mediterranean feel—more of a St. Tropez feel than a Mexican-American feel" says developer Jack Sommer. "I have no trouble deviating from the established regional architecture. This is Las Vegas."

The standard Las Vegas development is, like so many others throughout the country, fenced and gated—and each freestanding middle-class house is in most cases walled off from its neighbors. Such fortress domesticity, says University of Nevada at Las Vegas political scientist Bill Thompson, "makes it hard to see your neighbors. You don't even see your neighbors to say hi. A lot of people came here to start over, to change, and they don't want people attachments. Or rather they want to make their own people attachments, not to be thrown in with people just because their house is next door."

The problem with immersing so completely into one's own virtual reality is solipsism, a kind of holistic selfishness; other people don't matter unless they are players in one's own themed fantasy. It costs $150 a month just to keep a third of an acre green, and so the per capita water usage in Las Vegas is a gluttonous 343 gallons per day, compared with 200 in Los Angeles. The 702 area code has a higher proportion of unlisted numbers than any other. And although the per capita income is the 12th highest in the U.S., the electorate last year voted against building and improving parks. Officials say they need to build 12 new schools a year through the end of the century to accommodate the projected population influx, but they fear voters will decline to pay for them. Such civic disengagement is now a national phenomenon, but Las Vegas is at the cutting edge—and always has been. Back during the city's first spurt of urban hypertrophy in the '50s, when other new cities were grandly and confidently expanding their schools and social-welfare systems, Las Vegas was pointedly stingy.

Today's casino-driven prosperity is a somewhat self-contained bubble. The state's welfare case load has risen 54% just since 1991. "We currently have 10,500 new jobs coming online," says welfare administrator Mila Florence, referring to the staffing of the Luxor, Treasure Island and MGM Grand. "The number of persons coming into the state seeking those jobs far exceeds the number of jobs available, so our agency becomes the safety net."

Nor is it just social programs the locals are disinclined to fund. Last year voters defeated a series of bond issues that would have paid for 300 new police officers, seven new police substations, 500 new jail beds and improved security in the schools. Is the crime problem bad? Yes and no. Yes in the sense that the rates for murder and other violent crimes are somewhat higher than for the nation generally. But then they always have been—as is typical of resort areas, where tourists skew the figures. What's interesting is how even in its level of violence the rest of America has come to resemble Las Vegas. The city's homicide rate was 128% higher than the nation's as recently as 1982; today the Las Vegas homicide figure is only 56% higher than the national rate. In 1982 the local rate of violent crime—rapes, robberies, assaults, as well as homicides—was 90% higher than the national figure; today it is only 17% higher.

The theming; Liberace and Michael Jackson and Siegfried and Roy; the water gluttony; the refusal to build schools and police stations. It is fair to say that Las Vegas is in denial, which probably explains the local predilection for smarmy euphemism. From Wayne Newton on down, every man in Vegas calls every woman a lady. One of the local abortion clinics is called A Lady's Needs. Signs all over McCarran Airport declare it a nonsmoking building, yet just as noticeable as the banks of slot machines is the reek of old cigarettes. It strikes almost no one as ironic that the patron of the M.B. Dalitz Religious School is the late Moe Dalitz, the celebrated gangster.

It is understandable that the citizens are a bit embarrassed by their criminal founding fathers (Steve Wynn calls the Dunes "the original home of tinhorns and scumbags"), but the mixed feelings go beyond the mob. Last year Davy-O Thompson got zoning-board approvals to establish his haircutting salon, A Little Off the Top, where the female stylists were dressed in frilly teddies or paste-on breast caps and panties. But the board of cosmetology denied him a license an hour before he was set to open, citing concerns over "safety" and "hygiene." (He was eventually allowed to operate.) A similar protest contributed to the demise recently of a car wash featuring women in thong bikinis.

"We Las Vegans have been living under the stigma of Sin City for so long that we are desperate to prove that this is a very conservative, God-fearing, average American community that, just happens to have gambling," explains Under Sheriff Eric Cooper, who along with his boss, Sheriff John Moran, has been waging a 10-year antivice campaign. "The best thing that ever happened was when the Baptists had their convention here four years ago." The category of "Escort Services" is no longer listed in the local Yellow Pages.

It isn't just sex. Las Vegans are even ambivalent about gambling. Political discourse often revolves around keeping casinos away from decent people's homes. The promotional video produced by the Nevada Development Authority makes no mention at all of casinos. Even when a casino is a part of a new development, it is described as something else. Jack Sommer's Mountain Spa, the posh pseudo-Mediterranean resort about to start construction, will have a small "European-style" casino. But, says Sommer, "it's not really a casino. I call it a gaming amenity."

Semantic nuance, it turns out, is important. "They don't see themselves as gamblers," says Steve Wynn of the new tourists he is attracting. "They think of themselves as folks who are on vacation, and while they are there—hey, let's put some money in the slot machine." Wynn hired screenwriter Jim Hart (Hook, Bram Stoker's Dracula) to write a one-hour family-adventure TV movie (NBC, Jan. 23) set at Treasure island, and while Hart says the movie reaffirms family values and he flew his children out during production, he understands the place has an intrinsically dark edge. "You can come out for 24 hours and lose the tuition," he says. "There are a lot of desperate characters here."

For while the city is no longer the "Genet vision of hell" that John Gregory Dunne described in his book *Vegas: A Memoir of a Dark Season* 20 years ago, it is still, for the moment, a stranger place than Omaha or Sacramento or Worcester or even Atlantic City, if only because there are so many cheerfully offered temptations to lose the tuition and so many normal-looking people flirting feverishly with that risk. The mobs on the casino floors are in a kind of murmuring trance, each middle-aged housewife or young lawyer at the slots or the poker tables mentally grappling with a nonstop flow of insane hunches and wishful superstitions, continuously driven to unworthy leaps of faith that result in unwarranted bursts of self-esteem (Blackjack!) or self-loathing (Craps!).

Wynn understands the shadowy core of Las Vegas. "There will never come a day when [potential visitors] say, 'Should it be Orlando or should it be Las Vegas?' Those are two different moods. We think of our vacation in more romantic, personal terms. We're looking for sensual, extended gratification." In other words, Disney World is about tightly scripted smile-button fun for the kids; Las Vegas, despite the new theme-park accessories, remains the epicenter of the American id, still desperate to overpay schmaltzy superstars like Barbra Streisand, still focused on the darker stirrings of chance and liquor and sex.

If it is now acceptable for the whole family to come along to Las Vegas, that's because the values of America have changed, not those of Las Vegas. Deviancy really has been defined down. The new hang-loose all-American embrace of Las Vegas is either a sign that Americans have liberated themselves from troublesome old repressions and moralist hypocrisies, or else one more symptom of the decline of Western civilization. Or maybe both.

Excerpts from the Nevada Constitution

Some 18,000 words in length, the Nevada Constitution is three times as long as the United States Constitution. On March 21, 1864, Congress approved a bill enabling Nevada to become the 36th state to join the Union. The Constitution was ratified by delegates at a state convention in Carson City on July 28th of that same year, and Nevada was formally admitted into statehood by presidential proclamation on October 31, 1864, just in time for its three electoral votes to help Abraham Lincoln win reelection the following week. The fact that the Silver State was accepted into the Union during the Civil War explains the provisions prohibiting slavery and the assertion of "Paramount Allegiance" to the Federal Government.

Preliminary Action

Whereas, The Act of Congress Approved March Twenty First A.D. Eighteen Hundred and Sixty Four "To enable the People of the Territory of Nevada to form a Constitution and State Government and for the admission of such State into the Union on an equal footing with the Original States," requires that the Members of the Convention for framing said Constitution shall, after Organization, on behalf of the people of said Territory, adopt the Constitution of the United States.—Therefore, Be it Resolved, That the Members of this Convention, elected by the Authority of the aforesaid enabling Act of Congress, Assembled in Carson City the Capital of said Territory of Nevada, and immediately subsequent to its Organization, do adopt, on behalf of the people of said territory the Constitution of the United States[.]

Ordinance

Slavery prohibited; freedom of religious worship; disclaimer of public lands. In obedience to the requirements of an act of the Congress of the United States, approved March twenty-first, A.D. eighteen hundred and sixty-four, to enable the people of Nevada to form a constitution and state government, this convention, elected and convened in obedience to said enabling act, do ordain as follows, and this ordinance shall be irrevocable, without the consent of the United States and the people of the State of Nevada:

First. That there shall be in this state neither slavery nor involuntary servitude, otherwise than in the punishment for crimes, whereof the party shall have been duly convicted.

Second. That perfect toleration of religious sentiment shall be secured, and no inhabitant of said state shall ever be molested, in person or property, on account of his or her mode of religious worship.

Third. That the people inhabiting said territory do agree and declare, that they forever disclaim all right and title to the unappropriated public lands lying within said territory, and that the same shall be and remain at the sole and entire disposition of the United States; and that lands belonging to citizens of the United States, residing without the said state, shall never be taxed higher than the Land belonging to the residents thereof; and that no taxes shall be imposed by said state on lands or property therein belonging to, or which may hereafter be purchased by, the United States, unless otherwise provided by the congress of the United States. . . .

Preamble

We the people of the State of Nevada, Grateful to Almighty God for our freedom in order to secure its blessings, insure domestic tranquillity, and form a more perfect Government, do establish this Constitution.

Article 1, Sec. 1. Inalienable rights. All men are by Nature free and equal and have certain inalienable rights among which are those of enjoying and defending life and liberty; Acquiring, Possessing and Protecting property and pursuing and obtaining safety and happiness[.]

Article 1, Sec. 2. Purpose of government; paramount allegiance to United States. All political power is inherent in the people[.] Government is instituted for the protection, security and benefit of the people; and they have the right to alter or reform the same whenever the public good may require it. But the Paramount Allegiance of every citizen is due to the Federal Government in the exercise of all its Constitutional powers as the same have been or may be defined by the Supreme Court of the United States; and no power exists in the people of this or any other State of the Federal Union to dissolve their connection therewith or perform any act tending to impair[,] subvert, or resist the Supreme Authority of the government of the United States. The Constitution of the United States confers full power on the Federal Government to maintain and Perpetuate its existance [existence], and whensoever any portion of the States, or people thereof attempt to secede from the Federal Union, or forcibly resist the Execution of its laws, the Federal Government may, by warrant of the Constitution, employ armed force in compelling obedience to its Authority. . . .

Article 10, Sec. 5. Tax on proceeds of minerals; appropriation to counties; apportionment; assessment and taxation of mines. (Added in 1989.)

1. The legislature shall provide by law for a tax upon the net proceeds of all minerals, including oil, gas and other hydrocarbons, extracted in this state, at a rate not to exceed 5 percent of the net proceeds. No other tax may be imposed upon a mineral or its proceeds until the identity of the proceeds as such is lost. . . .

3. Each patented mine or mining claim must be assessed and taxed as other real property is assessed and taxed, except that no value may be attributed to any mineral known or believed to underlie it, and no value may be attributed to the surface of a mine or claim if one hundred dollars' worth of labor has been actually performed on the mine or claim during the year preceding the assessment. . . .

Article 11, Sec. 4. Establishment of state university; control by board of regents. The Legislature shall provide for the establishment of a State University which shall embrace departments for Agriculture, Mechanic Arts, and Mining to be controlled by a Board of Regents whose duties shall be prescribed by Law.

Article 11, Sec. 5. Establishment of normal schools and grades of schools; oath of teachers and professors. The Legislature shall have power to establish Normal schools, and such different grades of schools, from the primary department to the University, as in their discretion they may deem necessary, and all Professors in said University, or Teachers in said Schools of whatever grade, shall be required to take and subscribe to the oath as prescribed in Article Fifteenth of this Constitution. No Professor or Teacher who fails to comply with the provisions of any law framed in accordance with the provisions of this Section, shall be entitled to receive any portion of the public monies set apart for school purposes. . . .

Article 11, Sec. 8. Immediate organization and maintenance of state university. The Board of Regents shall, from the interest accruing from the first funds which come under their control, immediately organize and maintain the said Mining department in such manner as to make it most effective and useful, Provided, that all the proceeds of the public lands donated by Act of Congress approved July second A.D. eighteen hundred and sixty two, for a college for the benefit of Agriculture[,] the Mechanics Arts, and including Military tactics shall be invested by the said Board of Regents in a separate fund to be appropriated exclusively for the benefit of the first named departments to the University as set forth in Section Four above; And the Legislature shall provide that if through neglect or any other contingency, any portion of the fund so set apart, shall be lost or misappropriated, the

State of Nevada shall replace said amount so lost or misappropriated in said fund so that the principal of said fund shall remain forever undiminished[.] . . .